NATIONS OF THE WORLD

NIGERIA

Bridget Giles

www.raintreepublishers.co.uk
Visit our website to find out more information about **Raintree** books.

To order:
☎ Phone 44 (0) 1865 888113
▨ Send a fax to 44 (0) 1865 314091
💻 Visit the Raintree bookshop at **www.raintreepublishers.co.uk** to browse our catalogue and order online.

First published in Great Britain by Raintree, Halley Court, Jordan Hill, Oxford, OX2 8EJ, part of Harcourt Education Ltd.
Raintree is a registered trademark of Harcourt Education Ltd.

Produced for Raintree by the Brown Reference Group plc
Project Editor: Dawn Titmus
Designer: Graham Curd
Picture Researcher: Susy Forbes
Cartographers: Mark Walker and Peter Bull
Editorial Assistant: Tom Webber
Indexer: Kay Ollerenshaw
Consultant: Clive Carpenter

Raintree Publishers
Editor: Kate Buckingham

Printed and bound in Singapore.

ISBN 1 844 43244 0
08 07 06 05 04
10 9 8 7 6 5 4 3 2 1

British Library cataloguing in publication data
Giles, Bridget
Nigeria
916.6'9

A full catalogue is available for this book from the British Library.

Acknowledgements
Front cover: Nigerian man in a red hat
Title page: At mouths of the Niger River

The acknowledgements on page 128 form part of this copyright page.

Every effort has been made to contact copyright holders of any material reproduced in this book. Any omissions will be rectified in subsequent printings if notice is given to the publishers.

Contents

Foreword

S ince ancient times, people have gathered together in communities where they could share and trade resources and strive to build a safe and happy environment. Gradually, as populations grew and societies became more complex, communities expanded to become nations – groups of people who felt sufficiently bound by a common heritage to work together for a shared future.

Land has usually played an important role in defining a nation. People have a natural affection for the landscape in which they grew up. They are proud of its natural beauties – the mountains, rivers and forests – and of the towns and cities that flourish there. People are proud, too, of their nation's history – the shared struggles and achievements that have shaped the way they live today.

Religion, culture, race and lifestyle, too, have sometimes played a role in fostering a nation's identity. Often, though, a nation includes people of different races, beliefs and customs. Many may have come from distant countries. Nations have rarely been fixed, unchanging things, either territorially or racially. Throughout history, borders have changed, often under the pressure of war, and people have migrated across the globe in search of a new life or because they are fleeing from oppression or disaster. The world's nations are still changing today – some nations are breaking up and new nations are forming.

Nigeria is located in west Africa and has the largest population in the whole African continent. It is an ethnically diverse country, with some 250 different ethnic groups – all with their own language or dialect, culture and history. It is a land of abundant natural wealth, in the form of its oil reserves, but, at the same time, many of its people live in grinding poverty. For years, Nigeria was shackled by a military dictatorship that got rich on oil revenues while millions of Nigerians remained poverty stricken. Since 1999, however, and the restoration of civilian government, the country has been transforming itself into a democracy in which all Nigerians have hope for a prosperous future.

Introduction

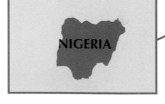

Located in west Africa, the country of Nigeria is a land of great diversity. It is also one of the most important countries, politically, economically and historically, in west Africa. It was here that the remains of the oldest civilization in Africa south of the Sahara were found. It is also home to some of Africa's most famous, beautiful and historic works of art. Known as the 'Giant of Africa', Nigeria has a greater population than any other nation in the African continent.

Nigeria is at the heart of the region. It is located at the bottom of the bulging western top half of Africa and almost exactly in the centre of the crook formed by the Bight of Benin. It is bordered to the west by Benin (formerly Dahomey) and to the north by Niger. Chad lies on Nigeria's north-east corner across the shores of Lake Chad, and Cameroon is Nigeria's eastern neighbour. To the south lies the Guinea coast, which borders on the Atlantic Ocean.

As in most African countries, many people make their living from the land, by farming, herding animals or fishing the rivers and sea. Yet not all Nigerians are farmers, herders or fishers. Many are officials, journalists, police and army officers, teachers, traders, doctors or business people. An increasing number live in cities and towns, some of which are hundreds of years old and among the oldest settlements in sub-Saharan Africa.

The city of Ibadan was one of the biggest in Africa by the 1800s. Today, it is the capital of Oyo state and Nigeria's second-largest city, after Lagos.

FACT FILE

- Among all the west African countries along the Atlantic coast, Nigeria is the largest. At 923,768 sq km (356,668 sq miles), it is almost twice the size of Spain.

- About 112 million people live in Nigeria, and several hundred different languages and dialects are spoken there.

- Like the USA and Germany, Nigeria is a federation. It has 36 states, each with its own capital and state government. The federal capital is Abuja.

- The capital of Nigeria used to be Lagos. It was moved to Abuja in 1991.

NAME, MONEY AND FLAG

Nigeria's official name is the Federal Republic of Nigeria, or Nigeria for short. It is named after the mighty Niger River, which flows from the north-west, south-eastwards across the country.

Since 1973, Nigeria's currency has been the naira. One hundred kobo make one naira. There are banknotes for 5, 10, 20, 50, 100, 200 and 500 naira.

The president is both the head of state and head of the government. After years of military rule, Nigeria is today making the transition to civilian rule.

The flag is made up of two equal vertical bands of green either side of a white vertical band.

The bands of green on Nigeria's flag stand for the importance of land and agriculture. The white band symbolizes unity and peace and the Niger River.

The 100-naira note depicts Chief Obafemi Awolowo, a Nigerian nationalist politician and leader of the Yoruba people.

THE PEOPLE OF NIGERIA

The people of Nigeria come from many different ethnic groups, each with its own history, culture, language and, often, religion. Broadly speaking, there are three main ethnic groups in Nigeria: the Yoruba, Igbo and Hausa. The Niger and Benue rivers form a huge Y shape across the country, dividing it into three regions: the north, where the Hausa and the Fulani live, the south-west, where the Yoruba live, and the south-east, where the Igbo live.

In actual fact, there are 250 documented **ethnic groups** and more than 400 linguistic groups in Nigeria. As well as the Yoruba, the Nupe and the Edo also live in the south-west. In the south-east live the Igbo, Ibibio, Efik and the Ogoni. Not only Hausa people live in the north;

POPULATION DENSITY

Most people live in the southern half of the country, especially in the south-east and in and around the city of Lagos, the former capital and the biggest city in Nigeria. In northern Nigeria, most people live in the Kano and Jigawa regions. The central, eastern and western regions are sparsely populated.

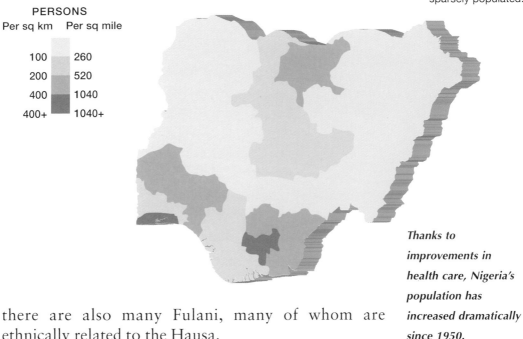

PERSONS

Per sq km	Per sq mile
100	260
200	520
400	1040
400+	1040+

Thanks to improvements in health care, Nigeria's population has increased dramatically since 1950.

there are also many Fulani, many of whom are ethnically related to the Hausa.

Many other smaller groups live in the mountain regions and around Lake Chad in the north-east corner. Some of these minorities number in the millions, such as the Kanuri of the north-east. Nigeria's tapestry of different peoples has emerged after centuries of intermarriage, migration, conquest and trade. It continues to change today as more and more people move to cities to live and work, leaving their ethnic homeland behind.

More than 20 per cent of all Africans and nearly half of all west Africans live in Nigeria, which is home to more people than any other

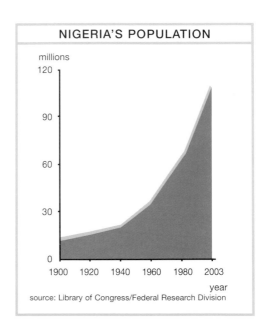

NIGERIA'S POPULATION

millions

source: Library of Congress/Federal Research Division

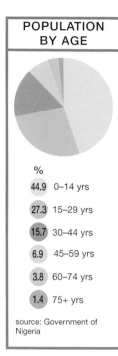

POPULATION BY AGE

%
44.9	0–14 yrs
27.3	15–29 yrs
15.7	30–44 yrs
6.9	45–59 yrs
3.8	60–74 yrs
1.4	75+ yrs

source: Government of Nigeria

Almost three-quarters of Nigeria's population are under the age of 30. Although people's life expectancy has improved in recent years, people in Nigeria generally die younger than people in Western and most Asian countries.

African country. The United Nations estimates that slightly fewer than 112 million people live in Nigeria, which is nearly twice as many people as the next most populous African country – Egypt.

In 1950, the fertility rate was 6.9 children per woman. Out of every 1000 children born, however, more than 180 died, and few people lived to be older than 40. The fertility rate continues to fall and today is about 5.1 children per woman. Since the death rate has also fallen and the average life expectancy is about 52 years, the population is still growing. Before 2030, some estimates say that Nigeria will have 200 million inhabitants.

In 1960, only 14 per cent of Nigerians lived in towns and cities. Today, almost 43 per cent live in urban and semi-urban areas. By 2020, it is estimated that nearly 60 per cent of Nigerians will live in towns and cities.

LANGUAGE AND RELIGION

Nigeria is one of the most complex countries in the world in terms of the number of languages and ethnic groups. Although people do not agree on the exact number, there are about 400 different languages spoken in Nigeria. In general, each is spoken by a different ethnic group.

Most Nigerians speak at least two languages fluently. As well as the language they learn at home, Nigerians learn to speak English at school. English is Nigeria's official language, used primarily in schools and for news, work, politics and business. Many people speak more than one African language, too. There are more Hausa speakers in west Africa than there are Hausa

WHERE DOES NIGERIA'S POPULATION LIVE?

43% cities and towns

57% countryside

National anthem

Nigeria's national anthem, 'Arise, O Compatriots', was adopted in 1978. The lyrics were written by a group of Nigerians, and the music was composed by Benedict Elide Odiase.

Arise, O compatriots,
Nigeria's call obey
To serve our fatherland
With love and strength and faith.
The labour of our heroes past
Shall never be in vain,
To serve with heart and might

One nation bound in freedom, peace
* and unity.*

O God of creation,
Direct our noble cause;
Guide our leaders right:
Help our youth the truth to know,
In love and honesty to grow,
And living just and true,
Great lofty heights attain,
To build a nation where peace and
* justice reign.*

people because Hausa became an important trading language hundreds of years ago. Today, Hausa is still widely spoken by people from different countries in Africa or ethnic groups who want to trade or do business together.

Half of all Nigerians are followers of **Islam** (**Muslims**), most of whom live in the north of the country, such as the Fulani and Hausa people. About 40 per cent of Nigerians are Christians. Christianity is most popular in the south of the country, among the Yoruba and Igbo people. Nigerian Christians are either Catholics (about 10 per cent) or followers of one of Nigeria's many independent Protestant churches (about 15 per cent). The remaining 10 per cent of Nigerians follow one of the African religions, such as the Yoruba or Igbo religion. However, many followers of both Islam and Christianity still follow aspects of their own, African, religions.

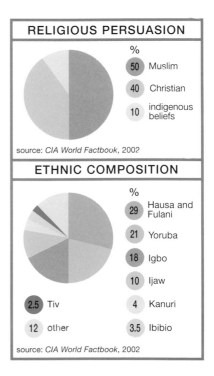

RELIGIOUS PERSUASION

%
50 Muslim
40 Christian
10 indigenous beliefs

source: *CIA World Factbook*, 2002

ETHNIC COMPOSITION

%
29 Hausa and Fulani
21 Yoruba
18 Igbo
10 Ijaw
2.5 Tiv
4 Kanuri
12 other
3.5 Ibibio

source: *CIA World Factbook*, 2002

Land and cities

*'The environment is man's first right.
We must not let it suffer blight.'*

Nigerian activist Ken Saro-Wiwa

When people think of Nigeria, they often think of Lagos – a busy tropical city. Once the capital city and still the largest city in the country, Lagos is, however, unlike the rest of the country. Nigeria is a land of diversity in terms of its climate, land, cities and people.

On Nigeria's south coast, there are wide coastal lowlands fringed by **mangrove** swamps or sandy beaches. Creeks wind inland through the swamps and into steamy forests beyond the coast. The vast Niger Delta, where the Niger River flows into the Atlantic Ocean, is a dense network of salty and freshwater creeks, streams and small rivers. In the south-east, near the border with Cameroon, are highlands.

Travelling north, into the heart of Nigeria, the Niger River valley is broad and shallow, bordered on either side by plateaux that get higher and higher. The forests are replaced by tropical grasslands (**savannahs**) with small trees and shrubs.

The Niger and Benue rivers meet in the centre of the country, forming a huge Y shape. Further north still, beyond the point where the Niger and Benue rivers meet, are the highlands and high plateaux of the north. The further north one goes, the drier it gets and the shorter the rainy season. Savannahs are eventually replaced by the semideserts of the Sahel, and across the border into Chad lies the vast Sahara Desert.

This market on Lagos Island specializes in food, crocks and baskets. Lagos has an abundance of markets, both on the mainland and on the islands.

FACT FILE

• The name 'Nigeria', after the Niger River, was suggested by British journalist Flora Shaw in the 1890s. Shaw later married Frederick Lugard, who was a governor of Nigeria when it was ruled by the British.

• Gorillas were rediscovered in south-east Nigeria in 1987. Before then, scientists thought that gorillas had died out in Nigeria.

• Nigeria's federal states were increased to twelve in 1967 and to nineteen in 1976, with Abuja as the new federal capital. By 1991, 30 states existed. In 1996, six new states were created.

THE TERRAIN

Three main types of terrain make up Nigeria. These are coastal lowlands, plains and highlands. The highlands include mountainous regions and high plateaux.

Coastal lowlands

Nigeria's coastline is far from smooth. It is jagged with inlets, bays, river mouths and lagoons. Lagoons are sea 'lakes' sheltered from the main ocean by barriers of sand or land. Along the coast are sandy, palm-fringed beaches or swamps. Where the rivers flow into the sea, and fresh water mixes with sea water, mangrove swamps often form. The largest of these swampy regions is the Niger Delta (see box on page 20). Further inland, the coastal lowlands become swampy in the rainy season (see page 23), and the mangroves are replaced by freshwater bogs.

Until recent centuries, the coast was separated from the inland plains by a broad band of forest. Today, many of the trees have been cut down for firewood or timber, and whole forests have been cleared for building on or farming. Stretches of rainforest and other types of forest still exist, though.

The shores around Lake Chad, in the far north-east corner, have some similarities with the coastal lowlands. This much smaller region has neither mangroves – because the water is not salty – nor many other trees – because there is not enough rain – but the land does get waterlogged during the rainy season, and swamps form.

Undulating plains

The plains (grasslands) are flat or gently undulating, like a gigantic rumpled sheet on a huge bed. In most of the country, the plains rarely reach higher than 500 metres (1640 feet) above sea level. Trees and shrubs grow in scattered thickets or alone, but there are never enough to form forests. Open woodlands were once common, but many have been cut down. The Sokoto

Ancient volcanoes surfaced the Jos Plateau with lava. Now extinct, the volcanoes have been worn away by the wind and rain, until only the sides of some remain. These craters collect rainwater and form lakes.

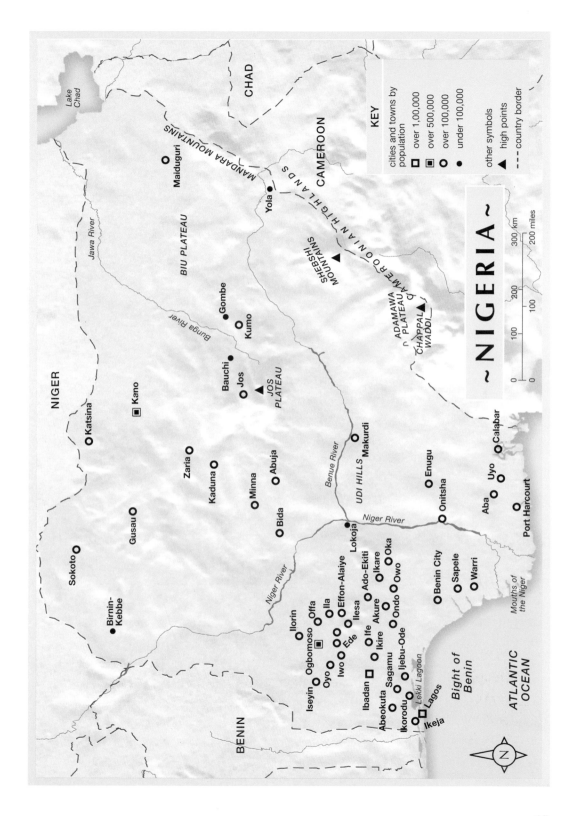

Plains are located in the north-west, and the Borno Plains are in the north-east. Much of Yoruba country, to the south-west of the Niger, is made up of plains.

The highlands

More than two-thirds of Nigeria are highlands. High plateaux rise in the centre, reaching more than 1500 metres (4900 feet) above sea level. The Niger and Benue rivers skirt around these central highlands' southern edges, and broad valleys cut shallow paths through the highlands. Hills and mountains dot the valley floors.

The Jos Plateau rises almost in the centre of Nigeria. It is the highest of the central highlands, reaching its highest point of 1781 metres (5843 feet) at Shere Hill. On average, it is 1280 metres (4200 feet) above sea level. Cliffs rise steeply from the Jos Plateau at places

NIGERIA'S LANDFORMS

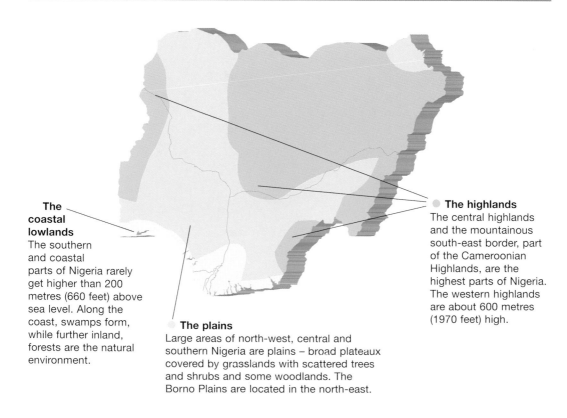

The coastal lowlands
The southern and coastal parts of Nigeria rarely get higher than 200 metres (660 feet) above sea level. Along the coast, swamps form, while further inland, forests are the natural environment.

The plains
Large areas of north-west, central and southern Nigeria are plains – broad plateaux covered by grasslands with scattered trees and shrubs and some woodlands. The Borno Plains are located in the north-east.

The highlands
The central highlands and the mountainous south-east border, part of the Cameroonian Highlands, are the highest parts of Nigeria. The western highlands are about 600 metres (1970 feet) high.

such as Udi-Nsukka. The highlands were once covered in forests, but dry grasslands have replaced the forests as more and more trees have been cut down.

The south-east region of Nigeria covers the mountainous foothills of the Cameroonian Highlands, the highest of which lie across the border in Cameroon. Those parts in Nigeria include the Adamawa Plateau and the Mandara Mountains. Most of these highlands rise steeply yet have smooth tops. Nigeria's highest peak, Chappal Waddi, is in the Gotel Mountains. It is 2419 metres (7936 feet) high.

The Jos Plateau in central Nigeria is mostly covered in grasslands, which have replaced the forests.

The rivers

The Niger River and the Benue River are the two most important rivers in Nigeria. The Niger rises in the Guinea Highlands, far to the north-west of Nigeria. Its journey to the sea is several thousand kilometres long. Along the way, the river passes north through Guinea

Onitsha on the Niger River is a busy commercial centre. Here passengers embark and disembark from ferries and wooden canoes.

and Mali, where it turns south by the edge of the Sahara Desert. Then, it flows through the southern tip of Niger, along the northern border of Benin and into Nigeria's north-west corner. The Niger completes its journey in the centre of Nigeria's coast, where it forms the spreading Niger Delta (see box on page 20).

At around 1083 kilometres (673 miles) long, the Benue is the Niger's longest **tributary**. It approximately doubles the size of the Niger. It flows from northern

Cameroon, Nigeria's eastern neighbour, into Nigeria across its north-eastern border. The Benue continues south-west until it joins with the Niger near the city of Lokoja, in Kogi state. There, the Benue is 1.6 kilometres (1 mile) wide, and the Niger about 1 kilometre ($^3/_4$ mile) wide. The meeting of these two mighty rivers creates a stretch of water that is almost a lake – one that is dotted with sandbars and small islands.

A large sandbar crosses the Benue, and the river water can sometimes be just 60 centimetres (2 feet) deep. Boats have to wait at Lokoja until rains swell the river enough to allow them to pass over the sandbar, and the return journey has to be made before the water level drops too far.

South of Lokoja, the Niger is confined to a narrow valley formed by plateaux to either side. In places, red-pink sandstone cliffs border the valley. The Niger emerges from its valley at Aboh, 200 kilometres (125 miles) north of the coast. There, the Niger separates into the many channels and branches of the Niger Delta. Every year, the Niger Delta floods – its creeks and streams begin to swell in August, reach their highest levels in October and return to normal in December. The floods can be controlled by opening and closing the Kainji Dam (see box on page 21).

In its upper reaches, the Niger River is steep and flows quickly. It drops over many falls in its rush down-hill and is frequently interrupted by rapids. The waterfalls on the Niger are not the only falls in Nigeria, however. Many rivers crash down the southern side of the Jos Plateau, which slopes sharply to the Benue River.

The Gongola River takes a slightly less steep route down the eastern side of the Jos Plateau. It flows north-east before turning south sharply and joining with the Benue River. The Gongola, too, has several scenic waterfalls. When there is little rain, however, the river almost disappears in places, and boats can no longer travel along it.

Many Nigerian rivers, such as the Kaduna and Gongola, start their journey on the Jos Plateau. The Kaduna is an important tributary of the Niger, and it accounts for 25 per cent of that river's flow after the two merge.

The Niger Delta

The Niger Delta is huge. Covering 36,000 sq km (14,000 sq miles), it is the largest delta in Africa and the third largest in the world. The Niger slows down as it flows through the low, flat coastal lowlands towards the sea. The slower waters no longer have the energy to carry the heavy loads of silt they have swept downriver. So the river drops its load on the river bed near its mouth. These deposits divide the river into a fan-like network of branches and build land where there once was sea. After millions of years, a giant wedge of land has developed that makes a 320 km (200-mile) bulge in Nigeria's coastline – the Niger Delta (see below).

Several of the 'channels' that lace the delta are rivers in their own right, such as the Nun, Forcados and Escarvos rivers. The Nun is 160 km (100 miles) long, and the Forcados is 198 km (123 miles) long. The delta continues to change as silt builds up. People keep the river routes open by regular dredging (removing the silt from the river bed).

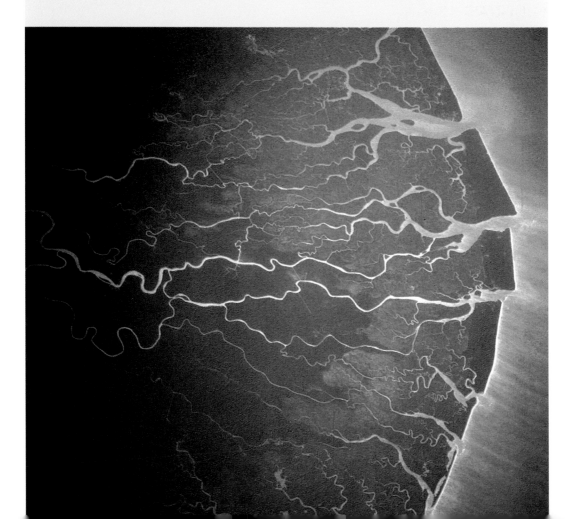

Kainji – dam, lake and park

In 1969, the Kainji Dam was opened, creating Kainji Lake on the Niger River in western Nigeria. The largest of the many dams on the Niger, Kainji Dam gives greater control over the river and its floods, as well as providing a route across the river and electrical power. The reservoir (Kainji Lake) provides water for crops and fishing. Its southern end is flanked by the two halves of Kainji Lake National Park. Families of baboons and packs of hyenas roam the savannahs, and hippos wallow in its rivers.

There was a price to pay, however. The 1300 sq km (500 sq miles) of land that now lie under Kainji Lake were once home to at least 50,000 people. The several historic towns and other settlements that these people lived in were flooded by the damming of the Niger. Most people were moved to resettlement villages near Kainji Lake.

NIGERIA'S STATES

Thirty-six federal states and the federal capital territory of Abuja make up the **Republic** of Nigeria. Each federal state has its own capital, where the state government is based. Some of the large northern states are based on historical Hausa city-states, such as Katsina, Sokoto, Kebbi, Borno and Zamfara (see pages 60–1). Oyo state includes much of what was once the Yoruba kingdom of Oyo (see page 53), and Edo state includes the capital of the historic kingdom of Benin (see page 55).

Some states are based around geographical regions, such as Plateau and Bauchi states of the central highlands; Niger state, which includes the Niger's floodplain before it merges with the Benue River; and Adamawa state, which covers the north-eastern highlands. Delta state covers most of the Niger Delta west of the river.

Smaller states cover the south-east region east of the Niger River. The land there was once heavily forested, but much of the forests have been cut down apart from in Rivers and Bayelsa states, on the delta, and Cross River state, on the south-eastern border. Delta, Edo and Ondo states have the most forested areas south-west of the Niger River.

THE STATES OF NIGERIA

Nigeria is divided into 36 states and one federal capital territory, Abuja. The map shows all the states and capitals (marked •), together with a list of their names. In 1991, the federal capital was transferred from Lagos to Abuja, where most federal government departments are now located.

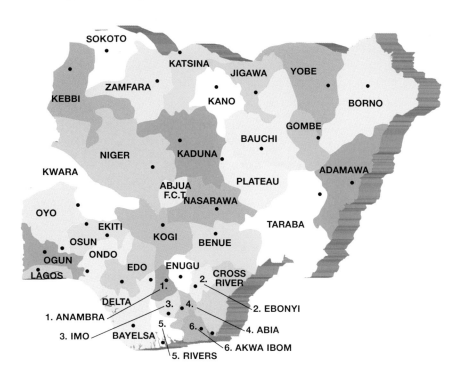

ABIA Umuahia	EDO Benin City	NASARAWA Lafia
ABJUA FEDERAL CAPITAL TERRITORY Abuja	EKITI Ado Ekiti	NIGER Minna
	ENUGU Enugu	OGUN Abeokuta
ADAMAWA Yola	GOMBE Gombe	ONDO Akure
AKWA IBOM Uyo	IMO Owerri	OSUN Osogbo
ANAMBRA Awka	JIGAWA Dutse	OYO Ibadan
BAUCHI Bauchi	KADUNA Kaduna	PLATEAU Jos
BAYELSA Yenagoa	KANO Kano	RIVERS Port Harcourt
BENUE Makurdi	KATSINA Katsina	SOKOTO Sokoto
BORNO Maiduguri	KEBBI Birnin Kebbi	TARABA Jalingo
CROSS RIVER Calabar	KOGI Lokoja	YOBE Damaturu
DELTA Asaba	KWARA Ilorin	ZAMFARA Gusau
EBONYI Abakaliki	LAGOS Ikeja	

Lagos state, Imo state and parts of Abia and Akwa Ibom states have the highest numbers of people per square kilometre. Other densely populated states are Oyo, Osun and Odon in the south-west; Enugu, Cross River, Ebonyi and Anambra in the south-east; and Kano and Jigawa in the north.

CLIMATE

In Nigeria, the climate varies from south to north. All of Nigeria lies within the tropics, but it is only the southern half that has a typically tropical climate. There, in the coastal lowlands and on the plains, it is nearly always hot and humid and there are two main seasons: wet and dry. Even during the dry season, it is still humid. The long rainy season (**monsoon**; see box on page 24) begins in February, April or March. The rains last for six to nine months, ending in October or November. Far more rain falls in the south-east than in the south-west, where the rainy season is longest.

Further north, the rainy season gets shorter and shorter, and the amount of rain that falls gets less and less. Temperatures also vary more between night and day and from season to season. The further north one goes, the colder it gets at night.

In the savannah, there are still distinct wet and dry seasons. There is less rain, however, and a longer dry season than in the coastal lowlands. In the semi-deserts of the far north, however, little rain falls at all. In much of northern Nigeria, there is just one short rainy season, lasting roughly from June to September. Most of the rain falls in July and August. The hottest months are April and May. Although lower than in the south, humidity is usually high, except when the harmattan winds blow (see box on page 24). These winds from the Sahara Desert bring very dry, warm air to the region. They are often accompanied by a haze that obscures the Sun.

In Lagos, on the south-west coast, the temperature remains fairly constant throughout the year, and rainfall peaks in June and July. Abuja, which is further north, has more variation in its annual temperature, and most rainfall occurs from August to September.

RAINFALL AND TEMPERATURE

Winds of change

Monsoons create Nigeria's wet and dry seasons. These seasonal winds change direction roughly every six months. Monsoons always blow from cooler to warmer regions. When the sea is cooler than the land, they blow inland. These winds carry water that they pick up from the sea and drop over the land, bringing the rainy season. When the land is cooler than the sea, the winds blow out to sea, producing a dry season on land.

At first, dry-season winds lead to clear skies, milder temperatures and lower humidity for most of Nigeria. By December, however, the winds are much stronger in the north, and they carry a load of fine dust from the Sahara. These winds, called the harmattan, blow across the whole of Nigeria – for more than three months in the north but for just two weeks in the south. At their worst, they obscure the skies and cover everything with a fine layer of dust, even inside houses. The winds are so dry that they suck moisture out of plants and stop them growing. The south is little affected by the harmattan. Once in a while, however, the winds are strong enough to reach as far south as Lagos and blow clouds of dust out to sea.

WILDLIFE AND PLANTS

Even though Nigeria is not famous for its animals – there are few lions and no zebras – it nevertheless has abundant wildlife. Since the 1980s, many new Nigerian animal species have been discovered as scientists study new areas, such as the Niger Delta. Each of Nigeria's geographical regions has its own particular plants and animals that are native to that region. The activities of people, such as farmers, builders, fishing people, miners and others, have either altered these natural environments or even helped create them.

Mangrove and freshwater swamps

Dense swamps, or thickets, of mangroves line parts of the coast, especially around the Niger Delta and the mouth of the Cross River in the south-east. The delta's mangrove swamps are the most extensive in Africa. In Nigeria, the largest and most common species (type) of mangrove is the red mangrove.

Nigeria's rivers and lakes contain Nile crocodiles, common hippos, a few manatees and a great variety of amphibians and fish, including several types of catfish and the tropical food-fish tilapias.

24

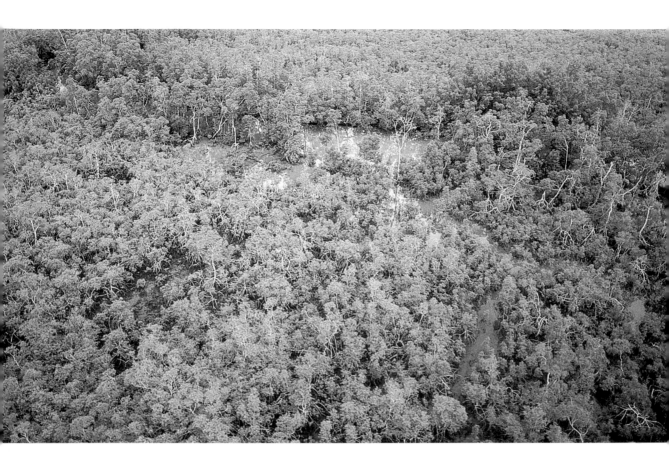

Mangroves grow between the high and low tide lines of sheltered creeks, deltas and lagoons. Few other plants can grow in salty water, but mangroves are able to get rid of salt through their leaves or filter it out through their roots. Having their roots covered by water kills most other plants, but red mangroves have prop roots, which start above the waterline on the trunk, where they can breathe. Other mangroves have knee roots, which poke out of the mud to breathe.

Behind the fringe of mangrove swamps, which can be up to 10 kilometres (6 miles) wide, lie freshwater swamps. The swamps of the Niger Delta form a large wedge that divides the mangroves from the lowland forests to the east and west. Elsewhere, freshwater swamps are not much more than a sliver between mangroves and lowland forest, if they are present at all.

Mangrove swamps and rainforest in the Niger Delta extend for 100 kilometres (60 miles) inland from the coast in some areas.

Mangrove swamps help build and protect coastal land. Their branching roots form dense networks that hold the silty seabed in place. The branches take most of the force of storm waves.

Papyrus and other 'floating grasses' edge swampy forests or form swamps themselves. Inland, grasses, shrubs and ferns grow before the taller trees of the true swamp appear. Many of the tall broad-leaved trees have buttress roots, which prop them up in the soft ground. The trees tend to be straight with relatively narrow trunks that are clear of branches until high up. African oaks, which can reach 50 metres (165 feet) tall, have no buttress roots but their bases are swollen. Shorter trees include raffia palms and abura (a hardwood seasonal tree). Oil palms line the rivers. Rattan vines festoon the branches of the trees, hanging in great loops and coils.

The savannahs

Although most savannahs are usually treeless, not all are totally free from trees. Woody savannahs have the occasional soaring idigbo tree, shorter bushwillows and thorny acacias, as well as tall elephant grasses, shrubs and herbs. The trees lose their leaves in the dry season, and many have thick bark that protects them from fire. Fire, both natural and started by farmers to clear land or flush out game, has helped create the savannahs.

Salty swamp life

The unique roots of mangroves form dense networks that provide habitats for many animals. The young of many species of fish, such as tarpon fry, as well as junior sea turtles, shrimps and lobsters prefer to spend their early years in mangroves. There, large, fast ocean-going predators such as dolphins and tuna fish cannot attack them.

Other animals spend their whole lives in mangroves. Oysters attach to the roots and filter food from the nutrient rich water. Rare west African **manatees** (sea cows) graze plants in mangrove swamps. Above the waterline, fiddler crabs scuttle over the mud flats when the tide is out. Talapin monkeys live in the branches. Crocodiles wait quietly for their prey. Hundreds of different types of birds live, feed and breed in the swamps. Many more thousands stop off in the mangroves as they migrate from their feeding grounds in southern Africa to breeding grounds in Europe.

Going north, woody savannahs turn into more open grasslands dotted with single trees. Trees such as the doum palm, tamarind, locust bean tree and acacias tend not to grow very tall and have wide, spreading crowns and narrow leaves. There are few broad-leaved trees in northern Nigeria. Baobab trees store water in their huge, swollen trunks, out of which spindly branches grow. Elephant grass – which can grow as tall as 4 metres (13 feet) – is replaced by shorter species that need less rain. In the far north of Nigeria, the savannahs become almost like deserts. During the dry season, nearly all the plants and grasses die back.

A few herds of savannah giraffes, buffaloes and elephants survive in national parks, but smaller animals are more common. **Warthogs**, **gerbils**, some antelopes and many birds live on or visit the savannahs. Vultures circle overhead on the lookout for carrion (dead animals) to eat, and stork-like secretary birds wade through the grasses on their long legs, stamping on the ground to flush out prey. Wild guinea fowl, the 'chickens' of west Africa, are also common.

Some of the savannah's most interesting residents are insects. Certain acacia trees are home to acacia ants.

A few solitary trees and shrubs dot the landscape on Nigeria's open savannahs.

27

Many Nigerians chew the twigs of the red ironwood tree, or false shea butter tree, to clean their teeth. This tree is common in woody savannahs.

The trees provide both food and shelter: the ants live inside hollow thorns and feed on nutritious buttons of protein and sugars that the tree provides. The tree benefits, too, since the ants defend their home by rushing out and biting animals attempting to eat the tree's leaves. Elsewhere, termites build towers of soil that they live inside in complex social groups.

Termites and ants attract other animals to the savannahs to feed, including **pangolins**. Pangolins have no teeth but use their long, thin tongue to sweep up ants and termites. They are covered in overlapping scales that protect and camouflage them. Some Nigerians use pangolin skin or scales in religious rituals and costumes.

The forests

North of the swamp forests, rainforests once covered the coastal lowlands. For hundreds of years, the land has been cleared for farming and allowed to regrow, and trees have been cut for firewood or timber, creating a patchwork of different forest types. To the Niger Delta's west, pockets and strips of rainforest interrupt more open parklands and seasonal forests, where there is not enough rain to support rainforests.

To the delta's densely populated east, large areas of the forest have been cut down, and between the delta and Cross River, there are almost no forests left. Some patches remain – in the Stubbs Creek Game Reserve and in a few, small sacred groves protected by local people. East of Cross River, however, are the largest and richest rainforests in Nigeria. There, the Cross River National Park protects the most abundant plant and animal life in Nigeria (see box on pages 32–3).

A visitor to a Nigerian forest might see birds feeding or nesting in the branches, many types of squirrels running up trunks and monkeys swinging from branch to branch. Colourful and not so colourful parrots are common. Grey parrots, with their bright red tails, constantly call to each other as they fly.

Forest night life

At night in the forest, cat-like **civets** and **genets** stalk smaller creatures, snacking on fruits and insects as they prowl. Forest genets live and hunt in trees; some west African forest genets eat nectar from trees. The crested genet is a rare species that lives in south-eastern Nigeria, largely in the Cross River National Park, and in the forests of Cameroon. The African palm civet lives in rainforests, where it spends much of its time in the canopy. Its cries can be heard at night, as males and females call to each other through the treetops. The African civet is bigger than the palm civet and lives in rainforests and on savannahs.

After the monkeys go to sleep, the big-eyed **pottos** and the angwantibos (golden pottos), such as the one below, come out to gobble up fruits and insects. These African bush babies cannot leap, and they move so slowly and smoothly that they are difficult to spot in their native habitat. If startled, they freeze or suddenly drop to the ground like a stone.

Other forest night life includes flying squirrels that glide from branch to trunk. In the delta and south-eastern forests, rare pygmy scaly-tailed flying squirrels catch insects and chew leaves. Night-flying birds include owls, such as the fishing owls of the swampy forests.

Monkey business

In forests east of the delta live Preuss's red colobus monkeys, crowned guenons and red-eared monkeys. Guenons are small, long-legged and long-tailed monkeys, some with markings. Red-bellied and Sclater's guenons eat fruit, leaves and insects, and never live far from water. Red-bellied guenons live in forests from the delta westwards. They look as though they have white beards and are also called white-throated guenons. Sclater's guenons live in forests along the lower Niger River, especially in the delta. They have been called Africa's rarest monkeys as fewer than 300 remain. Until both these types of guenon were rediscovered in Nigeria in 1988, people thought they had died out. A few groups of Sclater's guenons live near villages in sacred forests. These groups are protected by the local people, who consider them spiritual creatures linked to the gods. Elsewhere, they are hunted for their meat. Another monkey, the Niger Delta red colobus lives only in the delta forests.

While most ground dwellers are of the creeping and crawling variety – including thousands of species of beetles, spiders, centipedes and ants, for example – there are many bigger animals that live beneath the trees. Increasingly rare red river hogs, or bush pigs,

With their startlingly blue 'cheeks' either side of a bright red nose, male mandrills are unmistakable. Mandrills live in the south-eastern rainforests and spend most of their time on the forest floor.

snuffle the ground looking for tasty shoots. The forests also support several different types of antelope, each of which feeds on slightly different foods so that they rarely compete for their prey.

Antelope species

There are no large herds of antelopes in Nigeria, but many individuals live almost out of sight in the forests. **Sitatungas** live in freshwater swamps and marshy forests. Their long, pointed hooves splay out over soft ground and are attached to flexible feet, perfect for muddy ground. They can hide underwater with only their nostrils and eyes above water.

Nearly every forest is home to at least one type of the shy, secretive **duikers**. There are black-fronted, yellow-backed, blue duikers and grey duikers in Nigeria. These small or medium-sized antelopes live alone or in pairs, and blue duikers mate for life. They all browse on juicy shoots, leaves, fruits, buds and seeds.

Western **hartebeest, bongos** and **bushbucks** are large antelopes of the forest. They live in groups of fewer than ten animals. Western hartebeest live in more open forests and woodlands, where they graze on grasses and herbs. Bushbucks are common in both dense woodlands and savannahs. Bongos, the biggest of all the Earth's forest antelopes, prefer rainforests and are rare in Nigeria. A few may live in the Cross River forests. The spiral-horned bongos and bushbucks eat a range of plant foods, even digging up roots and tubers, breaking down hard-to-reach branches and gnawing tree bark.

Gorillas and chimps

Still bigger animals include the mainly ground-dwelling **mandrills**, chimpanzees and gorillas, as well as the largest forest dwellers – elephants and buffaloes. Gorillas are the rarest of all primates, and the Cross River gorilla, discovered in Nigeria in 1987, is the rarest of all gorillas. There are probably fewer than 200 Cross

The central African goliath frog, which lives in the Cross River rainforests, is as large as a human infant.

Nigeria's national parks

Nigeria's wildlife is under threat. Habitats are being destroyed to make way for farmland, roads, houses and businesses or, especially in the Niger Delta, to drill for oil. Forests are cut down for their timber or to use as firewood or building materials, while grasslands are trampled to death in the north. Most animals large and tasty enough to make a decent-sized meal are hunted by people.

Forests have long been logged for timber and firewood or patches cut down to create farmland without disappearing completely. Today, however, the size and poverty of Nigeria's population have pushed the hunting of wild animals, **desertification** and **deforestation** to unsustainable levels.

There is hope for the future, however. To protect Nigeria's plants and animals, several national parks have been set up. Most of Nigeria's national parks were established in 1991, but all of them existed before then as game or forest reserves. There is hope that more of Nigeria's reserves could be upgraded to national parks and therefore receive

CHAD BASIN

KAMUKU

KAINJI
LAKE

YANKARI

OLD OYO

GASHAKA-
GUMTI

OKOMU   CROSS
RIVER

greater protection. At the moment, some of Nigeria's most ecologically rich areas, such as the Niger Delta and the Jos Plateau, are not protected at all.

Jackals, giraffes, topi antelope, red-fronted gazelles and savannah elephants are all protected in the woodlands and grasslands of the Chad Basin National Park. Local people are allowed to farm the land, as long as they leave harvest leftovers for wildlife to feed on. As in most of Nigeria's parks and reserves, however, there are still problems with overgrazing and **poaching**.

Nigeria's few areas of untouched rainforests lie within the two sections of Cross River National Park, mostly on steep-sided valleys and cliffs. Popocarps and other trees grow in the cloud-drenched rainforests. Chimps, leopards, African golden cats and rat-like rock and tree hyraxes live in the forests, while baboons are more common on the savannahs. Several groups of western lowland gorillas as well as mandrills live in the Okwangwo division of the park.

Gashaka-Gumti National Park is perhaps one of the least explored areas of Africa. These high savannahs and mountain forests are home to chimps, elephants, olive baboons, several monkey species and even a few rare lions, giant forest hogs and hyenas. Hartebeest, bushbucks, kobs and waterbucks are common antelopes.

African buffaloes were once also common, but a disease passed on by cattle has killed many since the 1980s.

Nigeria's first national park, Kainji Lake National Park was created in 1975 from two game reserves. The park's woodland savannahs are home to savannah elephants as well as to lions, cheetahs and leopards. Duikers, hartebeest and kobs are common antelopes. Herds of waterbuck never stray far from water, and hippos wallow in the permanent waterholes. Nile and slender-snouted crocodiles lurk in rivers and the lake. Clawless otters and terrapin hunt the many species of fish.

To the north of Nigeria's largest cities – Lagos and Ibadan – lies the most accessible of Nigeria's national parks, Old Oyo. The savannah woodlands are home to elephants, buffaloes, hartebeest and duikers. The ruins of an ancient Yoruba city are preserved in the north.

The savannah woodlands of Yankari National Park are home to elephants, warthogs, lions, herds of antelope and the crystal-clear waters of the natural pool formed by Wikki Warm Springs. Marshall Caves, once inhabited by people, and the spectacular Borkono Falls are other places of interest.

Apart from national parks, there are also several game reserves and nature reserves. The nature reserves tend to be much smaller than the national parks.

River gorillas. They live in small groups of around five individuals led by the biggest male, the silverback. The gorillas spend their days searching for fruit, which they eat in great amounts, as well as leaves and the juicy stems of plants such as wild ginger. Gorillas rarely drink because they get most of the water they need from the plants they eat. Each night, they make a new nest to sleep in, using plants to make soft beds on the ground or on platforms made from bent tree branches.

Chimps live in both forests and savannahs of the south-east and south-west, spending hours every day looking for fruit, seeds and nuts. They use sticks to get tasty ants and termites out of their nests and sometimes even snack on small birds and reptiles.

Forest 'giants'

While there are no elephants or African buffaloes on Nigeria's savannahs – except in national parks – the forests are home to smaller cousins of these grassland giants. Small numbers of forest elephants live in the delta forests, rainforests and forest–savannah regions. As well as being smaller and darker than African

The blue duiker, a type of small antelope, lives in forests. Duikers are mostly nocturnal (active at night) and get their name from their habit of diving for cover when disturbed – 'duiker' is Afrikaans for 'diver'.

The high life

The southern slopes of the Jos Plateau have patches of rainforest that are home to some of the same plant and animal species as in the Cameroonian Highlands. The Cameroon horseshoe bat, the high-crowned bat and the dark-eared climbing mouse are all mammals that live in the Cameroonian Highlands and on the Jos Plateau and nowhere else in Nigeria. For this reason, it is likely that rainforests once covered what is now Nigeria all the way north to the Jos Plateau. The plateau is also home to many animals that live nowhere else.

Today, most of the plateau is covered with farmland or patches of savannah and rocky terrain, but there are no trees apart from along river banks. Larger mammals are not common because of the lack of cover and centuries-long human activity. Small Fox's shaggy rats live on the ground, while Nigerian mole rats burrow beneath. Both of these rodents are unique to the plateau. Barren-looking rocky areas free from human activity make good wildlife shelters, too. The west African **klipspringer** is a small antelope at home on steep, rocky land. Jos Plateau klipspringers are the only klipspringers in west Africa; far more klipspringers live in east Africa. Other species include Nigerian gerbils and Jos Plateau indigo birds, which lay their eggs in the nests of rock firefinches. The newly hatched indigo birds mimic the begging behaviour of young rock firefinches so that the step-parents feed them.

savannah elephants, forest elephants have straighter and thinner tusks and more rounded ears. Also, their tusks point down, not forwards, helping them to weave their way through tightly packed trees. As small herds of forest elephants march through a forest, they create paths that other animals, such as antelopes, can use.

Forest (dwarf) buffaloes live in south-eastern rain-forests, close to water and grassy glades where they can graze. With delicate features and narrow faces, they look more like red-brown dairy cattle than buffaloes. They like to wallow in mud and splash around in water but are not as placid as their domestic cousins. Forest buffaloes are powerful and deadly fighters, defending themselves fiercely. Several females and their offspring usually form groups of about ten to twelve animals.

CITIES

Nearly half of all Nigerians live in cities and towns. This is not a recent occurrence, however – hundreds of years before Nigeria even existed as a nation, Yoruba and Hausa people were living in towns. Historic Yoruba towns include Ile, Ibadan, Ijebu, Ogbomosho, Ilesha and Oyo. In the north, the Hausa people established several city-states, which are still regionally important today. Many have become state capitals, including Sokoto, Kano, Katsina and Birnin Kebbi. The delta and the south-east do not have such a long urban history. Bonny, Calabar and Brass were important trading depots in the 1800s. By then, Lagos and Ibadan were already among Africa's largest cities.

Lagos: a former capital

Over its 500-year history, Lagos has developed from a farming and fishing village to the largest city in Nigeria and one of the largest in Africa. Yoruba people have been living on Lagos Island, where Lagos city is based, since the late 1400s. Over the years, as international trade developed along the coast, Lagos grew into a trading centre, and more people came to live there.

The British took control of the city by force in 1861 so that they could control the trade that passed through its ports. Under foreign rule, Lagos was part of the British Gold Coast Colony (what is now Ghana) from 1874 to 1886, a separate state from 1886 to 1906, part of the Protectorate (colony) of Southern Nigeria from 1906 to 1914 and the capital of the whole colony of Nigeria from 1914. In 1960, when the country became independent from the UK, Lagos was made the capital of free Nigeria.

The whole of Lagos covers more than 200 square kilometres (77 square miles) of the south-west corner of Lagos Lagoon on the coast of south-west Nigeria. It is made up of three main islands – Lagos, Ikoyi and Victoria – and the surrounding mainland. The islands

Lagos harbour has three main ports: Apapa Quay and Tin Can Island, which are on the mainland, and Customs Quay, which is on Lagos Island. Apapa and Tin Can are where most goods enter and leave Nigeria.

are joined to each other and to the mainland by bridges, ferries, roads and railways. The swamps that once separated Ikoyi and Lagos islands have been filled in, but Five Cowrie Creek still separates Victoria and Ikoyi. The highest point on these low-lying islands is just 7 metres (23 feet) above sea level.

Ikoyi and Victoria islands are largely residential areas. There, rich Nigerians and foreign nationals live in large houses with substantial gardens, and foreign tourists stay in expensive luxury hotels. Many foreign diplomats live on Victoria Island, and several embassies are located there.

Lagos Island is the heart of the city. It is the site of the *oba*'s (king's) 200-year-old palace and the city centre. The north-western tip of Lagos Island, near the palace,

Lagos is spread out over 200 square kilometres (77 square miles), but the central part of the city is Lagos Island.

One of Lagos Island's many markets bustles with activity. The island is the commercial centre of the city and suffers from frequent traffic jams, which the locals call 'go slows'.

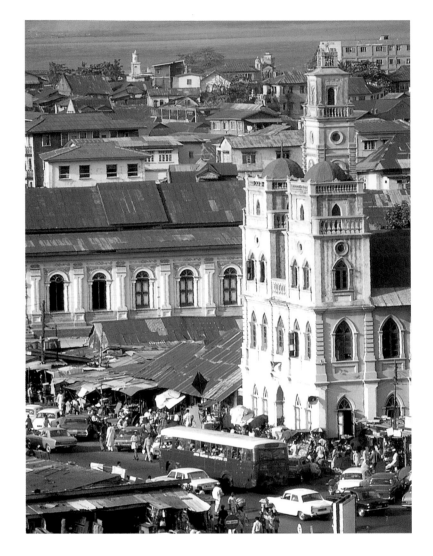

is where the first people to live on the island settled hundreds of years ago. Today, the narrow streets of the north and west are overcrowded with people, and the housing and facilities, such as water and electricity, are poor. Markets there tend to specialize in a variety of cheap goods and clothes (Jankara), food and baskets (Isale Eko) or cloth (Balogun). The Brazilian quarter in the centre of Lagos Island is a reminder of Lagos's links to the slave trade. The district was founded by freed slaves from the Americas and has some historic South American-style buildings.

Capital moves

Because Lagos was getting increasingly crowded, and because northern Nigerians complained that the south dominated government and politics, plans were made to move the capital of Nigeria in 1976. Abuja, in central Nigeria, began to be built with the aim of making it the new national capital. The change in capital has been gradual, and it was not until 1991 that the transfer was official. Some government offices still remain in Lagos but most have since moved to Abuja.

Abuja's landscaped streets are set against a stunning rocky backdrop.

The Central Mosque on the grid of streets formed by Independence Way North and South is almost dead centre in Abuja. The mosque and the grid of roads are within the central business district. To the north-east in Asokoro district are the buildings that house central government – the presidential complex and national assembly – as well as the supreme court and city hall. The other three districts of Abjua lie to the north and south of the business district. They are largely residential areas. Nnamdi Azikiwe International Airport connects Abuja with the rest of the world.

Port Harcourt is a sprawling city and the centre of Nigeria's oil industry. The first shipments of crude oil were exported from here in 1958.

The south-western shore of the island, along Marina and Apongbon streets, is the city centre and home to many businesses and the city's government and financial institutions. Skyscrapers, including Africa's tallest – NITEL House – pierce the sky, and many international firms and organizations are based there. Airline offices, as well as many cheap restaurants and shops, can be found at Tefawa Belawa Square at the western ends of Marina and Apongbon. Visitors to the Onikan National Museum, east of the city centre, can see Nigeria's history unfold from 3000 years ago to the present day.

Mainland Lagos

Murtala Muhammad International Airport is located on the mainland at the northern edge of greater Lagos. The University of Lagos, the central railway station, the National Theatre, National Gallery of Modern Art and a sports stadium are also on the mainland.

Northern Ikeju district is Lagos's administrative centre. Mushin and Shomulo are mainly Yoruba suburbs to the north of Lagos. At Mushin, there is a large industrial estate, where fabrics, shoes and powdered milk are made, and bikes and cars are put together. Farm products are traded in the large central market. In Shomulo, local businesses include leather handicrafts and printing. Mushin and Shomulo are overcrowded with poor housing and poor water and electricity supplies.

Port Harcourt

Port Harcourt is the capital of Nigeria's Rivers state and the centre of the country's oil industry. Set on the forested south-eastern coast, it is called the Garden City because of its abundant trees and parks. Now the second-most important port in Nigeria, after Lagos, Port Harcourt did not exist before 1913. In World War One (1914–18), soldiers left Nigeria from there to fight German forces in what is now Cameroon. The booming oil industry, which is focused on the delta, ensured the port's growth.

A huge flyover divides Port Harcourt into north and south. The old town, founded in 1913, is to the south, and the new town lies to the north. The trans-Amadi Industrial Area makes up much of the north-east. High-rise buildings and banks line the Aba Expressway. At the flyover, the expressway turns into Azikiwe Road, which is the centre of the old town.

Ibadan

Nigeria's third-largest city, Ibadan, is a sprawling metropolis. Originally a small settlement, it was launched into history by Yoruba refugees and rebels from the **civil wars** of the 1800s. It became the base of a powerful state before being conquered by the British at the end of that century.

Old town walls still stand around the Old Quarter in the south of the city. Within this quarter, the British built Mapo Hall on the highest point. Ibadans can now hire this former seat of colonial government for wedding receptions. Dugbe Market, although in the east of the city, is arguably the heart of Ibadan. A large market takes place there every day. The University of Ibadan and Transwonderland Amusement Park, Nigeria's Disney park, are on the north side of the city.

High-rise office blocks continue to line the route. Though crowded, the southernmost quarter is still charming. At its heart are Aggrey and Creek roads. A busy fish market is held on Creek Road.

Port Harcourt's southern half is surrounded on three sides by coastal inlets, and the town is a good base from which to explore local creek villages and towns. Within a few hours' boat journey are the two historic ports of Bonny and Brass islands.

Kano: capital of the north

Kano is the biggest and one of the most famous cities in northern Nigeria. Tradition states that it was founded in AD 999 or 998. Dala Hill, in the heart of old Kano, was already settled by the 600s.

CENTRAL KANO

Sabon Gari Market

MURTALA MUHAMMAD WAY

Syrian Quarter

KOFAR WAMBAI ROAD

Kurmi Market

Cloth Market

Dye pits

Old City

KOFAR MATA ROAD

OLD CITY WALL ALIGNMENT

STADIUM ROAD

RIMI MARKET ROAD

Railway Station

Grand Mosque

Emir's Palace

N

EMIR'S PALACE ROAD

Gidan Makama Museum

Formerly the largest of the ancient Hausa city-states (see page 61), modern Kano is Nigeria's second-largest city. The city has two main divisions, old and new. The walled old town makes up the western half. It has a wheel-like plan, with the city wall as the tyre, and the narrow roads as the spokes that radiate from Kurmi Market, which is at the hub. Kurmi Market sells local goods and crafts, such as richly embroidered Fulani horse blankets, leatherwork, textiles, metalware, beads and pottery. Market people sell their goods on stalls packed tightly in the maze of alleys. Dala Hill rises to the north of the market.

Although most of the 900-year-old city wall is ruins, some of the original city gates (*kofar*) have been restored. B.U.K. Road follows the wall's curve in the south and south-west, passing some good examples such as Kofar Na Isa (I Have Arrived) gate. Entering the old town from the west on Kofar Mata Road takes the visitor through a new *kofar* and past Kano's famous **indigo** dye pits. People still dye material there in much the same way as they have done for many generations. The pits are thought to be among the oldest in Africa.

Further west on Kofar Mata Road is the Grand Mosque. It is one of the largest mosques in Nigeria, and its towering **minarets** (small towers) offer spectacular views of the old city below. South of the mosque is the sprawling **Emir's** (**Muslim** prince's) Palace, an impressive example of Hausa architecture. The palace is not open to the public, however, because the emir still lives there. Opposite the emir's palace is a former palace that is open to the public – Gidan Makama Museum. It has exhibitions on Hausa architecture, history and arts.

New Kano, outside the city wall, contains the modern business district, which is defined by Murtala Muhammad Way and Airport Road. Sabon Gari (New Town) district to the north of Murtala Muhammad Way is home to many Yoruba and Igbo people, who are originally from the south of Nigeria.

Past and present

'For the African ... to make meaningful progress in the future, he [she] must not only appreciate but also appropriate his [her] cultural history.'

Nigerian **archaeologist** Bassey Wai Andah

Although Nigeria itself has existed only since the early 20th century, Nigerians share a history that stretches back many thousands of years. Historians once thought that Africa's story began with the arrival of Europeans – about 500 years ago in the case of Nigeria. Today, we know that Africa, and especially Nigeria, has a history of nation-building that began long before any Europeans arrived on Africa's shores. Studies of African oral history, which is passed down from generation to generation in stories, songs, poems and ceremonies, have revealed a rich and complicated past. There are relatively few documents detailing Africa's very ancient history, but scientific studies of languages, cultures, artefacts and settlements support and add detail to oral histories.

The earliest history of west Africa remains little understood, however. The hot, wet climate and acidic tropical soils preserve neither bones nor wood very well, and wood is one of the most important building material in forested regions such as Nigeria. Also, few archaeologists have been or are working in west Africa. Finding and studying promising sites is both time-consuming and expensive, especially if the land is covered by forests.

More recent history is easier to trace but complex because of the large number of states. Since the time of

This Benin bronze plaque depicts a noble figure. Hundreds of plaques such as this one used to adorn the walls in the royal palace in Benin.

FACT FILE

- In north-eastern Nigeria at the village of Dufuna, an 8000-year-old boat was discovered in 1987. It is the oldest boat in Africa south of the Sahara and one of the oldest in the world.

- The Nok culture, which was based around the central Jos Plateau, is the oldest known civilization in Africa south of the Sahara. It existed 2500 years ago. Some of the earliest evidence for iron-working in west Africa comes from the Nok.

- The conflicts between Nigeria's three main regions (north, south-east and west) stem in part from the colonial era.

In 2002, fossils of a 7-million-year-old skeleton were found in northern Chad, to the north of Nigeria. They belonged to a human ancestor who was about the size of a chimp but more human-like. Taoumi, as the skeleton was called, proves that our ancestors were more widespread in west Africa than previously thought.

Nok, the earliest civilization in **sub-Saharan** Africa, numerous kingdoms, city-states and empires flourished in what is now Nigeria. The arrival of Europeans changed the fortunes of many west Africans. Millions of people – many of them Igbo and Yoruba – were enslaved and shipped to foreign lands. Soon after the slave trade ended, it was replaced by foreign rule during the colonial era, when Nigeria itself was created. The effects of foreign rule are still felt throughout Africa today. However, independent Nigeria is set on a path to reclaim the future that was promised by its early history.

STONE AGE NIGERIA

The human history of Nigeria begins thousands of years ago, during the Stone Age, when people made tools and weapons from stone. In Africa, this period began about 2.5 million years ago and lasted until about 2500 years ago. At the start of the Stone Age, people were not the same as modern humans. They had smaller brains and had only just begun to walk on two legs.

Bones and stones

The oldest human fossils from Nigeria are those of a 10,000-year-old skeleton from Iwo Eleru near Akure in Ondo state. These are the bones of a modern human, not one of our earliest, ape-like ancestors.

Other evidence of Stone Age peoples, such as stones or animal bones with sharpened, chipped edges that were used as tools, dates from at least 12,000 years ago. Tools such as hand axes and cleavers were used for hunting, carving up meat, cutting plants and preparing food. Later, after people began farming, stone tools were used to dig irrigation ditches and prepare the land for crops. Stone tools up to 12,000 years old have been found on the Jos Plateau, at Afikpo in Imo state, Iwo Eleru, along the Taraba River in the north-east and the upper Sokoto River in the north-west and at Mejiro Cave near Old Oyo in the south.

ANCIENT SITES, KINGDOMS AND STATES

Prehistoric mounds

The north-eastern corner of Nigeria has many important Stone Age sites. For thousands of years, people built their homes on the same small areas of firm land that were not flooded by Lake Chad each year. After centuries, the remains of settlements covered again and again by soil developed into mounds. The remains of several-thousand-year-old settlements have been found at mounds at Ngala, Kursakata, Ndufu and Daima. North-east of the city of Maiduguri, along the shores of a long-dried-up lagoon fed by Lake Chad, pieces of pottery made by the resident hunters, fishing people and gatherers more than 4000 years ago have been found. At Ndufu, the remains of a house about 2800 years old lay within one mound. It is one of the oldest homes ever found in sub-Saharan Africa.

This map shows the location of some of the important ancient sites, towns, kingdoms and states in Nigeria.

The first farmers

At first, Stone Age peoples hunted animals for food and gathered fruit, seeds and nuts to eat. Over thousands of years, people learnt how to grow their own plants. This could have happened by accident: yams, an important root crop in Nigeria today, will sprout from the sour-tasting heads people leave to rot on rubbish heaps. Perhaps this gave the first farmers the idea of planting crops. Oil palms, another important crop, are also native to west Africa. They grow easily in open, wet forests and along rivers. These trees became so useful that people took seedlings with them when they moved to new areas. Oil palms provide palm oil, which is used for cooking and in palm wine, and the leaves are used to make roofing for buildings.

This terracotta head is from the Nok culture of the Jos Plateau. Nok figurines are the oldest examples of a well-developed tradition of sculpture in Africa south of the Sahara. For this reason, Nok has been called 'the birthplace of African art'.

Oil palms and yams are not the only crops that are native to west Africa, but they were among the first crops to be farmed there. Both were farmed in or near a west African tropical forest, perhaps as many as 5000 years ago. The site of this farming might have been Nigeria or Ghana. People were farming the fringes of forests in what is now Nigeria by 1000 BC.

Keeping animals

The only animal to be domesticated in west Africa is the guinea fowl – the so-called African chicken. Where the land was not suitable for farming, pastoralism (breeding and herding animals, mostly cattle) developed. In what is now Nigeria, this took place in the north. Cattle are not native to west Africa but were introduced from the north or east at several different times

The first ironworking people?

The spread of ironworking in Africa has long been linked with Bantu-speaking peoples. Bantu speakers came from the forested regions of what is now the Nigeria–Cameroon border. (Only a minority of present-day Nigeria's many languages are Bantu.) The Bantu spread from their homeland throughout much of central, southern and eastern Africa during the second or third millennium BC. However, many historians now dispute that the Bantu were solely responsible for introducing ironworking. The spread of Bantu speakers probably began before ironworking, and ironworking could have developed independently in several places in Africa at different times.

and places, perhaps as many as 9000 years ago. Rock paintings of cattle at Birnin Kudu near Kano and Geji near Bauchi may be 2500 years old.

IRON AGE NIGERIA

When west Africa's Iron Age began more than 2500 years ago in what are now Nigeria and Niger, great changes occurred. With stronger, more hard-wearing tools, people could clear and farm more land and trade any surplus they produced. They could also produce more lethal weapons to conquer other people and better defend themselves. The first towns emerged during the Iron Age, and some of the region's finest art was created.

Nok culture

In the 1900s, a tin miner working on the Jos Plateau near the village of Nok dug up a beautiful pottery head made from terracotta (baked clay). It was the first of several such figurines produced by an ancient iron-working people to be discovered. Nok figurines have since been discovered over a wide area in central Nigeria, stretching far south of Nok itself to cover much

Gifts from the dead

One especially rich grave at Igbo-Ukwu contained more than 166,000 items. These included mostly glass and stone beads but also more than 680 copper and brass items, and the bones of several skeletons. The metalware included jewellery, armour, sword hilts and a crown. All were superbly made and intricately carved. More ordinary items included iron nails and staples.

Five slaves were buried on top of what was a wooden chamber. Inside the chamber lay the remains of a man who was once of great importance. He wore a copper crown as well as a headdress studded with beads, a breastplate and strings of beads around his ankles and wrists. He carried a fly whisk, a symbol of authority in Africa. Having enough wealth for such an impressive burial suggests the society he lived in was very wealthy. Some people think he was the ruler of a kingdom in which all power lay with the king. Others think he might have been an important religious or spiritual figure to a farming people who believed the fate of their crops depended on his good fortune. Or he might have been a priest-king, which is somewhere between these two.

of southern Kaduna state. Nok art is famous worldwide for its artistic beauty and high quality. It is so well liked that many items have been stolen and smuggled out of Nigeria for sale to foreign art collectors. The society that created this art has been dubbed the Nok culture. Experts believe that the Nok culture existed from about 500 BC to AD 200.

Taruga, south of Nok village, is associated with the Nok culture. It is one of the oldest-known sites of iron-working in west Africa. Iron was produced there from 500 BC and perhaps even a few hundred years earlier. Several more recent ironworking sites have been found in Nsukka, south-eastern Nigeria, and elsewhere.

Nok smelters used furnaces with low shafts. Clay pipes blasted air into the furnaces, raising the temperature high enough to melt iron from its ore. Bellows might also have been used to blow air into the fire. The furnaces had a depression at their base for removing slag (molten waste).

Igbo-Ukwu

Like Nok, the next important site in Nigeria's history was also accidentally discovered. To the north of Owerri in south-east Nigeria, a man was digging earth to build a house. As he dug, he uncovered the first of many beautiful terracotta, bronze and brass artefacts. After more careful digging at the site, which was called Igbo-Ukwu, archaeologists uncovered a treasure trove. Dating from the 9th century AD, the goods were found in pits that turned out to be graves. So abundant were the buried riches, people assumed they had found the graves of long-dead Igbo kings (see box opposite).

The art of Igbo-Ukwu is the earliest-known metalwork from the whole of west Africa. It is of a different style, or tradition, from the arts of Nok, Benin and Ife.

THE FIRST CITIES

Ife was probably the first Yoruba town (see box below), and all the other Yoruba towns still consider it the most important. Other historical Yoruba towns include Ijebu, Oyo, Ilorin and Ibadan. While older west African cities have been unearthed, such as Jenne-jeno in modern-day Mali, the Yoruba have been described as, historically, the most 'urban' of all African peoples – for the number, importance and permanence of their cities. Some Yoruba states remain the oldest in west Africa's forested zone.

The origin of Ife

A Yoruba myth explains the origin of one of west Africa's first towns, Ife (where Ile-Ife in south-west Nigeria now lies). The myth says that before the Earth was created, the gods lived in the heavens above the sky, beneath which there was only water. One god, Obatala, grew bored, and he asked the chief god, Olorun, if he could create land for people and animals to live on. Olorun agreed, but Obatala was unsure how to do this. He went to ask another god, Ifa (or Orunmila), for help. Ifa helped Obatala create land. Obatala planted a palm nut in the new Earth where he first landed. He named the place Ife, in honour of the god who helped him create it. Later, Ife became the birthplace of humankind, and the offspring of Obatala founded other Yoruba towns.

Igbo society

The discovery of Igbo-Ukwu was surprising: Igbo society is often described as a 'stateless' one because the people ruled themselves. The Igbo of today have a saying about this, 'The Igbo have no kings'. Yet Igbo-Ukwu might prove that at least some Igbo people once had kings. Even today, an Igbo king, the Eze Nri, rules over a kingdom that has existed since before the 1600s. Though it was small, some Igbo remember the kingdom of Nri as the cradle of their culture. In the west, many Igbo people adopted the political structures of the nearby Benin or Yoruba kingdoms.

Elsewhere, however, the Igbo and many other delta peoples lived in villages or groups of villages led by councils. Men, women, elders, traders and other groups were represented at various councils, where decisions about trade, disputes and other matters were made. People who were rich, old, experienced or wise were chosen for the councils. In these ways, Igbo society rewarded initiative, achievement and age, rather than birth. In the north and west, though, Igbo chiefs governed by virtue of birth – that is, they were hereditary rulers.

Yoruba farmers lived in villages. Over time, neighbouring villages joined up. Eventually, towns and then cities emerged, each with a distinctive wheel-shaped pattern enclosed by walls. Some grew into important kingdoms and even empires. Many of the town dwellers were farmers, but plenty of people were traders, craftworkers, artists or officials. Farmlands lay outside the city walls, but farmers lived inside the walls.

Ife, the sacred city

Ife might have existed as early as the 10th century AD. It was at its height in the 1300s, when it was the capital of a kingdom, and many stunning works of art were produced. Its streets were paved with shards of pottery. The most famous and beautiful artworks were created for the court of the *Ooni* (king). Beautiful terracotta and brass heads might represent long-dead *Oonis*. Ife also specialized in the production of blue *segi* beads, which were glass beads that decorated the crowns of all *Oonis*.

The kingdom of Ife was eventually absorbed by a younger more powerful Yoruba kingdom, Oyo, which lay to the north of the forest region's edge.

Oyo

The Yoruba kingdom of Oyo existed by the 1300s. Present-day Old Oyo was its base, although there may have been other capitals at different times. The 1600s were a period of expansion for Oyo, which grew south to take advantage of trade with Europeans along the coast and to dominate the region.

Oyo's cavalry were vital in establishing the empire. Horses are not native to the region but were imported from across the Sahara. From these imports, the Yoruba bred small but hardy horses for use in battle. In the 1500s, Oyo had 1000 cavalrymen.

In the 1700s, Oyo was the most powerful Yoruba state, but its empire was torn apart in the 1830s by **civil war**. Ibadan and Ilorin emerged from the remains of Oyo, and, in turn, Ibadan became a powerful empire.

This copper mask from Ife may represent a long-dead Ooni.

Yoruba politics

Although the Yoruba states were ruled by kings, there were many checks and balances on their powers. The amount of power each king held varied at different times in each state. In all Yoruba states at all times, however, the king was an important religious figure and the central link between people and the gods. He carried out many religious ceremonies himself. Some gods, such as Sango, were once Yoruba kings.

In Ife, the *Ooni* was chosen from one of many branches of the royal **dynasty**, which had several thousand members. Once elected by the community, the *Ooni* went to live in the palace and was rarely seen

Nigeria's forgotten monument

Not far from Lagos lies Africa's largest single monument – Sungbo's *eredo*. The *eredo* is a massive moat 160 km (100 miles) long and 20 m (66 ft) deep in places. Its purpose is uncertain but it might have either marked the boundary of old Ijebu (one of the earliest Yoruba states), kept out elephants or been built to provide a home for protective swamp spirits. At more than 1000 years old, the *eredo* could prove that Yoruba states existed much earlier than experts originally thought. The moat is thought to have been dug for Bilikisu Sungbo, a powerful, childless widow whose grave is visited every year by thousands of Christians and Muslims, many of whom believe Sungbo was the biblical Queen of Sheba. Sungbo's state must have been well organized and wealthy to plan and dig the *eredo*. Unlike Sungbo's grave, however, the *eredo* is not protected and little is known about it. Experts fear it may disappear within twenty years.

again by his people. Palace officials, chosen from the ruling dynasty, and town chiefs carried out the *Ooni*'s orders and managed the kingdom.

Oyo was ruled by an *alafin* (king) selected by a state council from the ruling dynasty. At times, the *alafin* could appoint an heir to his throne, but the custom was for the crown prince to commit suicide on the death of the *alafin*. The *oyo mesi* (state council) was led by the *basorun* (prime minister). At times, the *basorun* held the real power in Oyo. An *oyo mesi* could even order the *alafin* to commit suicide.

THE KINGDOM OF BENIN

Benin is one of west Africa's most famous historical kingdoms. Its fame is partly due to the fact that a huge number of artworks and artefacts were looted from Benin City in 1897 by the British. These memorable pieces, including royal heads and more than 1000 bronze plaques, are now part of museum and private collections all over the world. Benin is also well known because it was in contact with Europeans since the late 1400s and the kingdom's history is well documented.

Benin was founded on the western half of the Niger Delta long before AD 1300. It was not a Yoruba kingdom; the founders were Edo speakers. However, legend says that a Yoruba prince or descendant of Obatala founded Benin. The *oba* (king) of Benin traced his power back to Ife. By the 1400s, Benin was an important power. Its position on the coast between the Igbo and Yoruba allowed it to grow rich through trade.

First European contact

In 1485, the Portuguese arrived on the coast and encountered the people of Benin for the first time. Benin and Portugal developed a close relationship at first. The chief of Ughoton (now the port of Benin) visited Portugal as an ambassador in 1485. Catholic missions were established by the Portuguese in Benin not long afterwards. In 1516, the *oba* ordered his son and two important nobles to become Christian. Members of the royal family learnt to speak Portuguese and also how to read and write.

Early Atlantic trade

The Europeans visited Benin to obtain things they could trade with the Akan of the Gold Coast (in modern-day Ghana). The Akan had plenty of one thing the Portuguese wanted – gold. Benin was close to the Gold Coast and was already a well-established and stable trading centre. The Portuguese exchanged brassware for cloth, beads – including glass beads from Ife – pepper and ivory.

The *obas* kept tight control over trade, in particular keeping slave trading to a minimum – slaves were needed to work in the kingdom. Benin refused to sell slaves to the Portuguese for nearly 200 years. The *obas*, for their part, wanted firearms, but the Portuguese refused to supply them. The Portuguese eventually found it easier to trade directly with the kingless Ijaw and Itsekiri to the south-east.

The historic kingdom of Benin in Nigeria has nothing to do with the modern country of the same name, which lies hundreds of kilometres to the west and was called Dahomey until 1975.

Trading from coast to desert

Trade was vital to the development of the states and self-ruled communities of what is now Nigeria. The people had been linked to long-distance trade routes for hundreds of years before Europeans arrived. Grave goods from Igbo-Ukwu that are 1200 years old were made from materials that were not available locally. These included glass beads that might have come from Venice, Italy, and copper from either the Sahara Desert, to the north, or the Congo, to the south. Getting copper from the Sahara linked Igbo-Ukwu to north Africa and also to Europe via the huge network of trans-Saharan trade routes (see map below). Goods reached Igbo-Ukwu from as far away as India or Persia (modern Iran).

Sixteenth-century Portuguese traders reported that the Igbo were part of a trading network that reached far inland to the north and west. Like other southerners, they sent salt and dried fish north, receiving farm products in return. They also traded metalware and other goods with people such as the Ijaw and Itsekiri, along the coast, and the Yoruba, to the west. In turn, the Yoruba traded goods such as cloth, ivory, peppers and palm oil with the Edo people in Benin, to their east.

Benin and the Niger Delta might have traded as far south as the mouth of the Congo River. Canoeists from what is now Ghana are said to have paddled that far in the 1600s, perhaps to get copper. En route, they would have passed the kingdom of Benin and the Niger Delta, where they probably stopped to restock and trade.

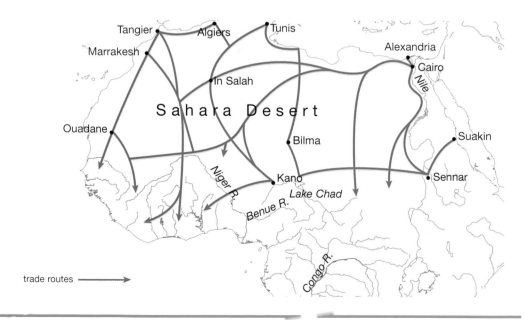

trade routes ⟶

Queen mothers

Women often held positions of power in west African states. For example, Oba Esigie of Benin created the role of *iyoba* (queen mother) for his own mother, Idia. She was given her own palace and ruled her own court as senior town chief. Hers was an important voice in palace affairs, even though she never saw her son again after he was crowned. Her vote or opinion had to be sought on all family and most political matters.

By the 1660s, the Portuguese trading posts, churches and missions had largely been abandoned. They were replaced by English and Dutch traders, and Benin started selling slaves to Europeans again in the 1700s.

The *obas* of Benin

In 1540, a Portuguese visitor said that the Benin kings '... are worshipped by their subjects, who believe they come from heaven. Great ceremony surrounds them.' Edo traditions trace the histories of more than 30 *obas* since Benin was first founded. The Portuguese met with the 15th *oba* when they first visited Benin. Oba Ewuare (ruled *c.*1440–73) was known as the empire-builder. He was responsible for rebuilding Benin City and founding many of Benin's political and administrative systems. He also conquered more than 200 settlements. Oba Esigie (ruled *c.*1504–50) created the office of queen mother (see box above) for his own mother. Under him, some of Benin's most famous court art was produced.

This Benin bronze head of a queen mother dates from the 16th century.

A depiction of Benin City by Olfert Dapper (1636–89), a Dutch physician and scholar who devoted most of his life to geographical studies without ever leaving his home town of Amsterdam.

Most of the famous 'bronzes' of Ife and Benin are actually made of brass. Some of the oldest Benin artefacts from the 1200s are real bronze, though.

Like the Yoruba kings, the *obas* of Benin had various checks and balances to limit their power. Originally, there were three sources of power in Benin: the *oba*, the *uzama* (king-maker) and the town chiefs. The *uzamas* were said to be descended from the founders of Benin. They chose and advised the *oba*. If an *oba* was considered to be a poor ruler, the *uzama* could order that he be killed.

The separate towns that made up Benin each had its own chief, who earned his position rather than inheriting it. These chiefs were led by the *iyase*, who was the *oba*'s main adviser. There was often friction between the *oba*, *uzama* and *iyase*, and the amount of power each group held varied from reign to reign. Oba Esigie established a fourth group of officials – the palace chiefs – to counterbalance the *uzama*. In addition to all these officials, craftworkers were organized into guilds.

Benin's final days

Benin began to get weaker during the 1700s, as people battled over the right to the throne and civil wars developed. The kingdom made much of its wealth from the slave trade, but that declined in the 1800s. Also, states to the north and west were pressing in on Benin's borders.

Finally, in 1897, the British ransacked Benin City, burning the *oba*'s palace and looting treasures. The British claimed that the attack was necessary to prevent Benin trading in slaves. Another reason was that Britain wanted to control Benin's trade. The *oba* was deposed (removed from the throne), and six officials were executed. Many of Benin's magnificent artworks were stolen and given to museums around the world or sold to meet the costs of the attack on Benin. After 1897, Benin was made a part of British Nigeria and was governed indirectly through a council of chiefs.

THE NORTHERN STATES

The north of Nigeria has a history that is as complex as that of the south. Myths (stories) trace the origin of many states to Arab heroes who came from the Middle East across the Sahara Desert. While these stories might or might not be true, they reveal the importance of links to lands north of the Sahara.

Trade with desert-living peoples and Arabs who crossed the Sahara Desert helped turn many kingdoms into wealthy and important states. Traders imported horses, weapons, salt, copper and north African pottery; the Hausa and others exported cloth, leather, slaves, gold and ivory. Exports were produced locally or traded for with people living to the south. The Hausa were particularly good at leatherwork; gold came from the Akan people in what is now Ghana.

These 17th-century bronze figures on spikes, male (below) and female (left), used to be inserted into the ground on either side of the oba.

Human sacrifice?

When the British attacked Benin in 1897, they found the remains of hundreds of men and women sacrificed to the Edo gods. Trees with human corpses tied to them could be seen throughout the kingdom, and burial pits containing scores of bodies were later uncovered. Benin was called the 'city of blood' as a result. Yet reports of cruelties may have been exaggerated to justify the British attack. And historians are unsure whether or not human sacrifice was common practice and for how long. Some think that the grisly sacrifices increased as the power of Benin declined. The *obas* struggled to keep their power by plying their gods with gifts, and the sacrifices may also have kept fearful subjects loyal. The ritual was not new, though. Forty-one young women were found buried in a mass grave in Benin that dates from the 1200s.

Islam in the north

It was not only goods that were brought across the desert by traders. The **Islamic** religion made the journey, too, from Arabia and north Africa, where it was well established. It had a great influence on what is now the north of Nigeria. **Muslims** were probably living in the region by AD 1000, although few of the northern states were then Islamic. The Hausa city-states, as well as Borno, Borgu (now partly covered by Lake Kainji) and Sokoto all became important Islamic states. Their cities and towns were home to Muslim scholars and clerics. Several became important centres of Muslim learning and culture.

Kano is one of the more famous Hausa true towns because of the 'Kano Chronicle'. This 19th-century Arabic document records the history of Kano from early times.

The seven true towns

According to tradition, a hero named Bayinjida became *sarki* (king) of Daura after killing a monstrous snake and marrying the queen of Daura. Their children are said to have founded the seven true Hausa towns, or Hausa *bakwai*. These are Biram, Daura, Gobir, Kano, Katsina, Rano and Zazzau Zaria (also called Zegzeg and today Zaria). Other Hausa towns, the *banzai bakwai* (worthless ones) trace their origins to the grandsons of

Africa's longest earthworks

Benin was surrounded by massive earthen walls, earthworks and moats that total 16,000 km (10,000 miles) long. These extensive earthworks (called *iya*), cover more than 2590 sq km (1000 sq miles). The only larger human-made structure on the Earth is the Great Wall of China. The earthen mounds enclose patches of land that might once have been smaller towns and villages that were swallowed up by Benin. The *iya* date from the 1200s to the 1400s, but some parts date back to the early 8th century AD.

This carved ivory salt cellar from Benin represents a Portuguese seaman in a ship's crow's nest. It dates from the 17th century.

Bayinjida by a mistress (concubine). The *banza bakwai* include Gwari, Kebbi, Jukun, Yawuri and Zamfara.

By AD 1000, several Hausa *bakwai* existed, and by 1350, many had become city-states. Each city was independent, but at times some were more powerful than others. Zazzau was most powerful in the late 1500s under Queen Amina. By then, most Hausa towns were ruled by **emirs** (Muslim rulers). Today, many of the northern emirs are still influential figures in modern-day Nigerian politics.

The ruling classes of the Hausa city-states often included people of Fulani origin. Historically, the Fulani were cattle herders who came to the north from the Senegal River valley. Fulanis had been moving into the Hausa region since the 1200s. Some settled in the towns, where they formed an educated, religious Islamic elite. They worked as advisers, Islamic judges and teachers. Other Fulani remained outside the city walls, herding cattle and travelling in search of fresh pasture and drinking water.

This wooden board in the Hausa style is inscribed with Qur'anic text (from the Muslim holy book). The Hausa city-states became important Islamic states.

Islamic revolution

The Hausa states were united into one nation in the 19th century by a Fulani jihad. 'Jihad' is an Arabic term that means 'holy struggle', although often it is defined, misleadingly, as 'holy war'. 'Jihad' refers to the struggle that every Muslim makes to bring him- or herself closer to Allah (God). This struggle can, sometimes, include bringing Islam to non-Muslims or warring with non-Muslim states.

By the start of the 1800s, after twenty years of teaching in Gobir, Fulani Muslim scholar Usman dan Fodio (1754–1817) gathered a large following of Muslims. He wanted Muslims to adopt Shari'a (Islamic) law, overthrow unjust rulers and wipe out non-Islamic practices. Dan Fodio's followers included educated urban Muslims as well as pastoral Fulani, ordinary Hausa people and slaves. The popular revolt he began in 1804 in the northern Hausa town of Gudu led to similar uprisings in more than 30 Hausa towns. The **emirates** dan Fodio and his followers set up were loosely joined under the authority of newly established Sokoto. By the 1850s, the empire was the largest in west Africa. Uprisings inspired by Sokoto spread Islam throughout the whole northern region of west Africa. Dan Fodio retired in 1811 and was succeeded by his son Muhammad Bello (1781–1837).

THE SLAVE COAST

The people of what is now Nigeria were greatly affected by the slave trade with Europeans, which reached its height during the mid-1700s. Many Yoruba and Igbo people, in particular, were enslaved. Others, such as Oyo, Benin and some delta people, supplied slaves to the Europeans. The introduction of firearms from Europe and the incentive of receiving valuable goods in exchange for slaves led to more and more wars and raids to capture slaves. Oyo, for example, was often at war with its neighbours.

It is difficult to know what impact the sheer numbers of people lost to slavery had on the region. However, the slave trade must have at least weakened states by depriving them of huge numbers of people's labour, learning and experience.

Olaudah Equiano

As a boy in Igbo country, Olaudah Equiano (*c.*1745–97) was captured by slave raiders near Benin in 1756. He was taken across the Atlantic to the island of Barbados in the Caribbean and then to Virginia in the USA. He earned the price of his own freedom by careful trading and saving. He went to London, where he converted to Christianity and became a leader of the abolitionist movement.

In 1789, Equiano published his memoirs, *The Interesting Narrative of the Life of Olaudah Equiano, or Gustavus Vassa, the African*. This book became a bestseller, making Equiano a wealthy man. He was one of the first African novelists, and his book is an important source of slave trade history.

Olaudah Equiano
or
GUSTAVUS VASSA,

A cruel and inhuman trade

'The closeness of the place, and the heat of the climate, added to the number in the ship, which was so crowded that each had scarcely room to turn himself, almost suffocated us … the air soon became unfit for respiration, from a variety of loathsome smells, and brought on a sickness among the slaves, of which many died …. This wretched situation was aggravated by the galling of the chains, now become insupportable; and the filth of the necessary tubs, into which the children often fell and were almost suffocated. The shrieks of the women, and the groans of the dying, rendered the whole a scene of horror almost inconceivable.'

This description of the slave hold on a slave ship was published in 1789 by Olaudah Equiano, an Igbo man and a former slave (see box on page 63).

Slavery and slave trading existed in west Africa before the arrival of Europeans. Prisoners of war, debtors and convicts were often enslaved. But slaves could also be part of people's families, and some held offices of great power.

However, never before the Atlantic slave trade had slave trading been carried out on such a huge scale or in such a cruel manner. Slaves were packed into ships like sardines in a tin. This chart, for example, illustrates the stowage on the slave ship *Brookes*, which carried 422 slaves on the lower deck. Hundreds died of diseases or starved in these overcrowded conditions before they reached the Americas. Those who resisted or were troublesome during the crossing were dumped overboard.

Racist theories about African peoples emerged, as though they were breeds of animals rather than simply people of different backgrounds. The Igbo, for example, were said to be easy to control though moody and prone to suicide.

Once they reached their destination, the Africans were sold like goods at slave markets. Then, a life of hard work and cruelty awaited them. Some slaves saved

enough money to buy their freedom. The majority of slaves, though, were not this fortunate. Many were born into slavery and most died in captivity

Samuel Ajayi Crowther

Samuel Ajayi Crowther (1809–91) was a Yoruba man who was sold into slavery at the age of twelve. Rescued by a British navy patrol before he reached the Americas, Crowther was taken to Sierre Leone. There, he became a Christian. He returned to Yoruba country in the 1840s as a missionary. He became the first black bishop, in the Niger region, and wrote several important studies of Yoruba language and history.

From the early 1500s, Europeans had been colonizing lands in Central and South America. They wanted cheap labour to work their mines and crop plantations in their colonies. After many of the local Native American populations had been killed by imported diseases and overwork, the Europeans turned to Africans as a source of labour. By the 1600s, England, France, Denmark, the Netherlands, Portugal, Spain and Sweden were trading slaves along the west African coast, from modern-day Senegal to Angola.

Initially, the Portuguese were the most important slave traders, but later they were replaced by the Dutch and then by the French and British. Britain was the most important slave-trading nation in the 1700s. American ships joined the trade by the 1800s, transporting slaves to the USA to work on plantations in the south.

Delta slavers

Oyo was one of west Africa's key slave-trading nations. Exports of slaves from Oyo reached about 20,000 per year between 1680 and 1730, and the Bight of Benin became known as the Slave Coast.

After Oyo collapsed after civil war in the 1830s, delta people controlled slave trading in the region. The coastal towns of Bonny, Calabar and Elem Kalabari were major slave exporters. They received slaves from inland traders and sold them to Europeans. Igbo and

British ships patrolled the Slave Coast from the mid-1850s. They searched ships for slaves and freed captives at Freetown, Sierre Leone.

65

Ibibio people belonging to the Aro clan supplied most of the slaves to these ports (clan members have a common ancestor). The Aro had long acted as mediators of local disputes, and the sacred grove of their god at Arochukwu was a court of appeal for many people, not just the Aro. Because of their influence, Aro traders could travel widely without fear of attack.

A 'triangular trade' was established that took manufactured goods to west Africa from Europe; slaves from there were taken to the Americas; and tobacco, cotton, molasses and rum were imported from the Americas to Europe. This Atlantic slave trade resulted in more than 10 million west Africans being taken from their families; 3.5 million of these came from what is now Nigeria.

Abolition of the slave trade

In Europe and the Americas during the 1700s, the growing antislavery (abolitionist) movement was joined by many freed slaves, such as Olaudah Equiano (see box on page 63). Abolitionists believed that slavery was morally wrong, yet economic arguments probably had more to do with bringing an end to the trade.

This print depicts English missionaries arriving in Nigeria in the mid-19th century. Like the explorers before them, European Christian missionaries helped open up west Africa to foreign rule from the 1840s on.

The increasingly industrial Western world needed markets for its goods more than it needed slaves.

France outlawed slave trading in 1794 (and then again in 1818), Denmark in 1803, Britain in 1807, the USA in 1808, Sweden in 1813 and the Dutch in 1814. Slavery and the slave trade continued after the trade had been outlawed, however, because many states had become dependent on it. Also, as long as the Americas needed slaves to work on their plantations, the trade continued. Slavery was finally abolished in all British territories by 1834 and was made illegal in the USA in 1865.

COLONIAL RULE

The end of the slave trade was closely followed by the colonial era, when European nations set up colonies throughout Africa. The British colonized what is now Nigeria. The reasons for colonial rule are many and complex. As the slave trade came to an end after the 1860s, trading in goods became more important again.

The Industrial Revolution began in England in about 1750 and spread to other Western nations. This economic revolution was triggered by the invention of powered machines that allowed the mass production of cheap goods in factories. As the revolution took hold, it led to a search for cheap raw materials to make the goods from and for new markets to sell the goods to. Africa was seen as an important supplier of both.

From trading to colonizing

In the lands of present-day southern Nigeria, palm oil became the most important trade good. This oil was used in Europe to lubricate machinery and to make soap. People of the Niger Delta dominated this trade, so their lands were known as the 'oil rivers'.

In the late 1800s, there was a world economic depression, with low economic activity and high unemployment. The price of goods fell sharply. Palm oil, for instance, dropped from around £155 per barrel to less

Kanem and Borno

Borno in the north-east corner of Nigeria was once a province of the mighty Kanem empire, and later an important state itself. Kanem was most powerful in the 1200s, when it stretched nearly as far as the north African coast. In the 1400s, however, its people and rulers sought refuge from invaders in the empire's southernmost province, Borno. Under Mai (**Sultan**) Ali Gaji (died 1503), the people re-established their empire, even retaking Kanem. The heart of the revived state remained in Borno, though. Under Mai Idris Alooma (1569–1603), Borno became the most powerful empire in west Africa and a centre of Islamic learning and scholarship.

In 1808, Fulani jihadists drove the *mai* from his capital, Birnin N'gazargamo. An Islamic scholar named El Kanemi helped the *mai* reclaim his throne in 1837. El Kanemi became more powerful than the *mai*. Using the title *shehu*, he ruled Borno alone after 1846. Today, the emirate of Borno in north-eastern Nigeria is an important reminder of Borno's past.

than £80. The profits of African and European traders fell. At the same time, rivalries between European nations spilt over into Africa. To continue making profits and stop other Europeans 'stealing' their trade, many argued that they needed to take control of the trade and trade routes themselves. At the Berlin Conference of 1884–85, European nations agreed on 'spheres of influence' in Africa. Britain laid claim to the Niger Basin, among other regions. Claims had to be made good by occupation and foreign rule, establishing colonies.

The Royal Niger Company

The economic need for colonies was demonstrated by the fact that many were established by businesses. The Royal Niger Company (once the independent United Africa Company), for example, was responsible for colonizing much of Nigeria on behalf of the British government. The British used both treaties (agreements between independent nations) and force to get their way. Treaties were often earned by deceit, however. Such treaties were signed with Sokoto, Oyo, Ijebu and

Benin by 1885. The African rulers did not realize or were not informed that they had signed away control of their empires. But British opinion differed. Force was often used to make sure that the terms of the treaties – as understood by the British – were kept to. Benin and the Yoruba states were conquered by 1897.

Delta resistance

Resistance to British control was widespread, and was especially successful among the Igbo and other delta peoples. In 1885, the British declared a colony, the Oil Rivers Protectorate, in the delta. The local people's knowledge of the terrain allowed them to adopt **guerilla tactics**, however, hiding out in the forest and attacking quickly before troops could prepare. The British had to

This 20th-century carved relief panel on a palace gate depicts the arrival of the British district commissioner – a reminder of the days of colonial rule. Artists working in the Yoruba tradtion often carve scenes from everyday life on door panels of important buildings.

European exploration

From the 1790s, Europeans began to travel inland beyond the coast of west Africa for the first time. They had rarely ventured inland before. Explorers such as Scotsman Mungo Park (1771–1805) wanted to find out where the Niger River began and ended. Park followed the river for more than 1500 km (900 miles) but drowned in rapids under what is now Lake Kainji in 1805.

Another Scottish explorer, Hugh Clapperton (1788–1827), visited the Sokoto **caliphate** in 1822–24 and was convinced that the delta was the river's mouth. It was Clapperton's servant Richard Lander (1804–34) and Richard's brother John (1807–39) who proved what Clapperton had learnt, though. The Lander brothers were captured by slave traders and sold downriver to a European ship.

The expeditions of such explorers discovered nothing that Africans did not already know about their land. Their trips did, however, provide others with useful information that was vital to the European traders and the establishment of colonial rule.

conquer each self-ruled village one by one. Oil Rivers was renamed the Niger Coast Protectorate in 1893.

In 1899, the Royal Niger Company lost its royal charter, which allowed it to act on behalf of the British government. The British appointed Frederick Lugard as high commissioner of the Protectorate of Northern Nigeria, which the company had loosely established over Sokoto, other Hausa states and Borno. Lugard's task was to take fuller control. Borno did not resist, but attacks were launched on Kano and Sokoto in 1903.

In the south, the conquered peoples and states were joined as the Protectorate of Southern Nigeria in 1906. In 1914, Southern and Northern Nigeria were combined as the Protectorate of Nigeria.

Lagos had been annexed (taken over) by the British as early as 1861.

Indirect rule

Lugard was responsible for the introduction of indirect rule. This policy granted Africans the right to self-rule within the rigid control of the British government, represented by the governor general.

In northern and south-western Nigeria, many emirs and kings remained. The complex political systems of the Yoruba and Benin kingdoms were not well understood by the British, however. In the south, legislative councils were set up to advise the governor of each region. Most of the council members were British. In the south-east, warrant chiefs with no historical claim to power were appointed and were very unpopular. Rebellious rulers would be replaced by less troublesome ones.

One of the most unpopular colonial policies was the hut (poll) tax. This was levied on every person in the colony, and it forced people to earn cash working in the British mines or factories or to grow **cash crops**. There were many revolts against this tax.

The British also organized the building of roads and railways and the dredging of harbours, at times using forced labour. While this helped certain regions to develop, it also led to hostility, since northern Nigeria was not developed as much as the south.

The road to independence

From the 1920s, Nigerians began campaigning for increased political rights and independence. Many of the emerging political parties drew their support from a particular **ethnic group**, even if their leaders wished to

The 1929 Women's War

In 1929, Igbo and Ibibio women waged war against symbols of British power. They marched in their thousands and destroyed British factories and the native courts of the warrant chiefs. The women hated colonial rule because they had lost their voice in local affairs with the introduction of warrant chiefs. The British had assumed that the men spoke for the women in political matters, as they did in Britain. That was not the case among the self-ruled communities of the south-east, however.

The British ruthlessly suppressed this popular uprising, or 1929 Women's War, shooting dead at least 500 demonstrators at Egwanga Beach, Opobo, in December of that year.

attract all Nigerians. Among the Yoruba, Herbert Macauley and Chief Obafemi Awolowo were important figures; among the Igbo, Dr Nnamdi Azikiwe was prominent; and in the north, it was Tafewa Balewa. Nigerian women such as Funmilayo Ransome-Kuti took active roles in this struggle, setting up political groups and organizing protests. When Nigeria finally became independent from British rule in 1960, Balewa was prime minister.

INDEPENDENT NIGERIA

In 1963, Nigeria became a federal **republic**. President Azikiwe replaced the UK's Queen Elizabeth II as head of state, and Balewa remained in charge of the government as prime minister. Nigeria's first period of independent democratic rule lasted six years.

In those years, there was much conflict between and within the south-west, south-east and north. To great outcry, Chief Awolowo was found guilty of **treason** and imprisoned. The results of two censuses, which decided the number of seats a region has in parliament, were hotly disputed, and many riots broke out. Promising to

The Biafran War

In 1967, Colonel Ojukwu, the military ruler of the eastern region, refused to accept the authority of Nigeria's new military leader, a young Christian named Yakubu Gowon. In the north, soldiers were still killing Igbos. Between 5000 (according to official reports) and 30,000 (according to Igbo reports) were slaughtered. More than a million Igbos returned to the south-east. One year later, Ojukwu declared the independent Republic of Biafra to, he claimed, protect the Igbo. Fierce fighting broke out as the government's troops tried to regain control. The Igbo were outnumbered and outgunned, but their morale was high. They preferred surprise attacks and raids behind enemy lines. Biafra's food and medical supplies were blocked by Gowon's troops, however. Resistance finally collapsed in 1970, after a huge army assault. By then, up to 3 million Biafrans had been killed in the conflict or died of starvation or disease.

restore order, the army assassinated key politicians and overthrew the government in 1966.

Military rule

The army **coup** (takeover) was led by Igbo officers, and northerners feared that the Igbo were trying to take over the country. As many as 7000 Igbos living in the north were massacred, and 500,000 fled to the south-east. Within months of the first coup, another group of army officers – this time led by northerners – killed the army general and took control of the country. Within a year, Nigeria was plunged into civil war (see box opposite).

This pattern of coup and counter-coup continued for years in Nigeria. Further coups occurred in 1975 (twice), 1983, 1985 and 1993. For a short period, **democracy** replaced military rule during the Second Republic of 1979–83. Concerns about 'squandermania' under President Alhaji Shehu Shagari, when politicians amassed fortunes as the ordinary people's standard of living fell, led to riots. Again, the army took control.

British colonial administrators are photographed here in the early 20th century in Lagos. They are meeting with tribal messengers from the interior of Nigeria.

73

Nigerians celebrate the re-election of prime minister Tafewa Balewa's party to power in December 1959. The election took place ten months before Nigeria gained its independence from the UK.

The leader, Major-General Muhammad Buhari, promised to restore order, stamp out corruption and rebuild the economy. He arrested many corrupt officials but also many of his critics.

Turbulent times

Buhari was overthrown by officers led by Major-General Ibrahim Babangida in 1985. Babangida promised to return the country to civilian rule but postponed elections several times. People were unhappy with Babangida's regime, accusing him of human rights abuses. When presidential elections finally took place in 1993, it looked as though Chief Abiola, a Muslim from Yoruba country, was certain to win. Some people disagreed, however, and Babangida stepped in to declare the elections invalid. In Lagos, hundreds of civilians staged pro-democracy demonstrations, and the troops were called out. Unexpectedly, Babangida stepped aside and set up a temporary civilian government. Riots over the price of fuel and a general strike broke out, however, and General Sani Abacha took power within a few months.

Between 1993 and 1998, Abacha banned political parties, arrested his critics, dissolved all elected bodies and controlled the press. Millions of pounds of oil money was stolen by government officials and politicians. Within Nigeria, campaigns for democracy increased, despite the restrictions. Many demonstrations turned into riots when faced with the army's heavy-handed tactics. Abroad, governments and political leaders, including the former South African president Nelson Mandela, called for Abacha to step down. Revolts in Ogoniland caught the attention of the world, especially when activist Ken Saro-Wiwa was executed in 1995 (see box on page 86).

Abacha promised to allow elections in 1998. Months before they were due, he died of a heart attack. People celebrated in the streets, even though his death delayed the elections. In the words of Nigerian novelist Wole Soyinka (see page 107), they 'were sick of military rule'.

Elections finally took place in 1999. They were won by Olusegun Obasanjo, remembered as the only military ruler to hand power back to the people (in 1979). President Obasanjo and the ruling People's Democratic Party (PDP) were re-elected in 2003.

NIGERIA TODAY

Nigeria is a federation, like Germany and the USA. There are 36 states, plus the federal capital territory of Abuja, each with its own state government and capital. In addition to federal and state governments, there are also local governments.

At the federal level, two houses make up the National Assembly (parliament) – the House of Representatives (the lower house) and the Senate (the upper house). The National Assembly makes federal law. Members of

Before Olusegun Obasanjo was sworn in as president in 1999, he made a world trip that included Asia, Europe, the USA and much of Africa, demonstrating that Nigeria was back on the world stage after years of military dictatorship.

The Nigerian National Assembly (parliament) consists of two houses - the Senate (upper house) and the House of Representatives (lower house).

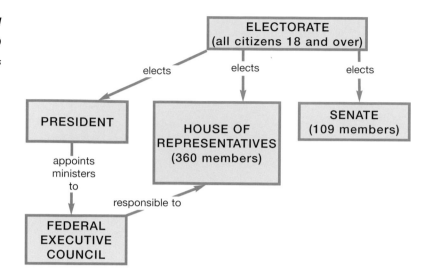

parliament (senators and representatives) and the president are elected for four-year terms.

The 36 states are divided into 360 federal constituencies. Each constituency elects one member to the House of Representatives. All Nigerian men and women aged eighteen and over have the right to vote in presidential and state elections.

THE NIGERIAN NATIONAL ASSEMBLY IN 2003

Head of state and of government: President Olusegun Obasanjo (since 29 May 1999)

Senate

109 seats • last election 2003 • elections held every 4 years

People's Democratic Party (PDP)	53.6%	
All People's Party (APP)	27.9%	
Alliance for Democracy (AD)	9.7%	
others	8.8%	

House of Representatives

360 seats • last election 2003 • elections held every 4 years

People's Democratic Party (PDP)	54.5%	
All People's Party (APP)	27.4%	
Alliance for Democracy (AD)	9.3%	
others	8.8%	

In the 2003 general elections, President Obasanjo's People's Democratic Party was re-elected to power with a large majority.

President Obasanjo is pictured here making a speech in Calgary, Canada, in 2002. He was attending a meeting with other world leaders, including the British prime minister, Tony Blair (back row, third from left), and U.S. president, George W. Bush (back row, second from right).

The four most important political offices are, in order, the president, vice-president, Senate president and speaker of the house. The president governs with a federal executive council (Cabinet) made up of about 30 ministers. The Senate president is head of the Senate, which is made up of three elected senators from each state and one from the federal capital territory of Abuja, making 109 in total. The speaker of the house heads the House of Representatives, which is made up of 360 elected members, one from each constituency.

The economy

'An anthill that is destined to become a giant anthill will definitely become one, no matter how many times it is destroyed by elephants.'

Nigerian proverb

Nigeria has one of the biggest economies in Africa. It has abundant natural resources, such as oil and natural gas, a labour force that numbers at least 66 million people and the largest home market in **sub-Saharan** Africa. Oil is crucial to the Nigerian economy. It accounts for more than 90 per cent of Nigeria's export earnings and for about 80 per cent of government earnings. As Africa's biggest oil producer and the world's 14th largest, Nigeria pumps 2 million barrels of crude oil on to international markets every day. About 41 per cent of it is imported into the USA.

The wealth created by the oil industry is not evenly spread around the country or among Nigeria's people, however, and Nigeria is among the poorest countries in the world. The reasons for this are complex and linked to both the world economy and to Nigeria's recent and not-so-recent history. Dependence on the sale of oil –

FACT FILE

• Unemployment was estimated to be 28% in 1992. By 1997, it had dropped to 3.2%.

• In 2002, Nigeria's **gross national product** (GNP) per person was £200. In the same year, the UK's GNP per person was £14,800.

• In 2003, £1 equalled 213 Nigerian naira.

• Nigeria's central bank (CBN) estimates that the economy grew by 3.3% in 2002.

• Inflation is estimated to have slowed to 14.2% in 2002, compared wtih 18.9% in 2001.

• In 2000, Nigeria's foreign debt was 84% of its GNP.

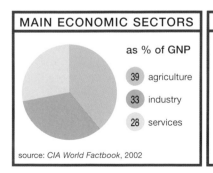

MAIN ECONOMIC SECTORS

as % of GNP

39 agriculture
33 industry
28 services

source: *CIA World Factbook*, 2002

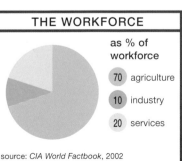

THE WORKFORCE

as % of workforce

70 agriculture
10 industry
20 services

source: *CIA World Factbook*, 2002

Women wash clothes in a muddy river in the oil-rich delta region. Despite the wealth generated by oil, most local people remain very poor.

An economic history

An understanding of Nigeria's past is necessary to understand Nigeria's economy. Since the colonial era (see pages 67–72), Nigeria's economy has been closely controlled by officials, politicians or military leaders. This situation has not always been of benefit to Nigerians.

Colonial rulers were more interested in making the colony profitable for its foreign rulers than developing an independent economy that could survive the ups and downs of the world market. Under British rule, the country's age-old ties with traders to the north and elsewhere were broken. This process began long before with the slave trade (see pages 63–7).

As a colony, Nigeria became dependent on supplying the world market with cash crops, such as cacao, palm oil, groundnuts and cotton. Taxes forced people to grow crops for sale. The colony's goods were exported as raw materials. Bigger profits are made from turning raw materials into goods, such as cotton into cloth, than are made from selling the raw materials themselves. The British did not want to deprive their home-based factories of this profitable income, however, so manufacturing industries within Nigeria were discouraged. When Nigeria became independent, its economy was dependent on the export of raw materials. Even since the discovery of oil in 1956, Nigeria's mostly military governors have been unable to break this dependency. Today, Nigeria is dependent on exports of crude ('raw') oil.

and, to a much lesser extent, **cash crops** such as cacao and rubber – has weakened Nigeria's economy in the long term. The prices of raw materials go up and down markedly on the world market. Price slumps can have disastrous effects on economies dependent on one or two raw materials, such as Nigeria's.

Although industry creates one-third of Nigeria's GNP, only about 10 per cent of the labour force work within that sector. Manufacturing accounts for only 4 per cent of GNP. Agriculture is hugely important in Nigeria. Seventy per cent of people make their living in that sector, which creates 39 per cent of GNP. Twice as many people work in services than in industry, yet the service sector accounts for a smaller proportion of GNP.

Farm workers in Kano stack sacks of groundnuts. Groundnuts are an important crop in the north.

AGRICULTURE

The majority of Nigerians make their living from the land, either by growing crops or herding animals (pastoralism). Fishing is also an important activity, especially on the delta and along the Niger. Many of the farmers, herders and fishers produce a small surplus that they either sell at local markets or trade for goods with neighbours. Farms are generally small, and the growing of both food and non-food crops is done largely by small-scale farmers tending just a few hectares.

More than 30 per cent of Nigeria's land is either used to grow crops on or as pasture for animals. Most of the farmers live in the south of the country. People who make their living herding animals are concentrated in the north. In the south-east and around Kano, Katsina and Sokoto, farming land is in such short supply that large numbers of people have moved elsewhere to find land. A lot of pasture and farmland in the north of the country has been lost to the process of **desertification.**

Along river valleys, in broad and shallow hollows and around Lake Chad, farmers take advantage of

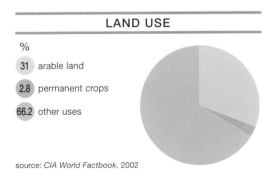

LAND USE

%
31 arable land
2.8 permanent crops
66.2 other uses

source: *CIA World Factbook*, 2002

81

HOW NIGERIA USES ITS LAND

Large areas in the south around the Niger Delta are wetland or rainforest. Crops are grown in many parts of the country, while much of the central and eastern parts of Nigeria are given over to pasture.

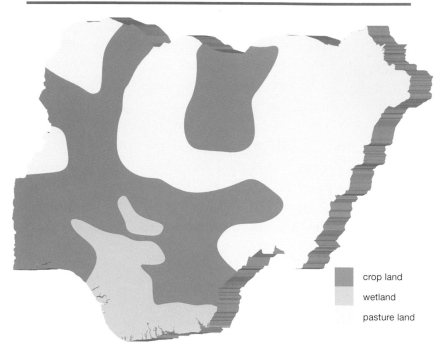

crop land

wetland

pasture land

seasonal floods to grow crops or graze animals. This is called *fadama* (floodplain) agriculture. In the north, farmers build **shadoofs** to irrigate their land. These ancient devices are buckets attached to weighted wooden poles that raise river water to the land.

Foods and non-foods

In the south, root crops are the most important food crops. These include yams, taro (or cocoyams), sweet potatoes and cassava (or tapioca). In the drier north, grains are more common. As well as maize, drought-resistant sorghum and millet are grown. Rice is grown anywhere the land is wet enough, and black-eyed beans are a staple in the north. African rice has largely been replaced by imported Asian varieties.

Other important crops are palm oil, cacao and rubber, in the south, and groundnuts and cotton in the north. Cocoa and chocolate are made from cacao, which is an important export crop.

Herders and breeders

There are more than 10 million cattle in Nigeria, probably even more sheep and twice as many goats. Most of these animals are owned by individuals or villages rather than by commercial farms. Farmers and herders keep sheep and goats throughout Nigeria, but most of them are kept in the north. In the south, some farmers keep a few pigs, but few farmers do in the largely **Islamic** north (**Muslims** do not eat pork). Nearly everyone, in rural areas at least, keeps chickens.

The Fulani of the north still dominate cattle-herding, producing most of the country's beef. Kano and other northern cities are also known for their leatherwork.

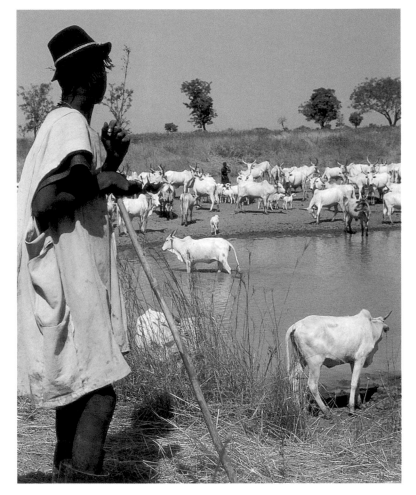

A Fulani herder with his herd of cattle at a waterhole. Most of Nigeria's cattle herders are Fulani people from the north of the country.

The 'Moroccan' leather sold in Europe and noted for its quality actually comes from Sokoto. Most cattle in the north are zebu, which have a distinctive hump on their back. The Fulani keep large herds of zebu, along with many goats and sheep. Their herds often include cattle owned by town dwellers, who pay the Fulani to care for their animals.

TRADE

Trade is vital to Nigeria's national and international economy. For hundreds of years, the north and south of what is now Nigeria have exchanged goods. This trade still continues within the country today. Plantains, cassava, kola nuts and fruit travel from south to north. Beans, onions, leather goods and livestock travel from north to south. There is also a lot of trade between towns and cities and between urban and rural areas. Rural farmers and herders bring their crops or livestock to markets in nearby towns. Women, especially in the south, have long played important roles as market traders, shopkeepers and street hawkers, and many markets are dominated by women.

Exports and imports

Nigeria's most important international trading partners are not other west African states but the USA and Europe. Nearly half of all the goods Nigeria exports goes to the USA – the vast majority is crude oil and crude-oil products such as petroleum.

EXPORTS (£000 m)		IMPORTS (£000 m)	
oil	11.8	manufactured goods	1.7
non-oil	0.1	machinery and transport equipment	1.4
total	11.9	chemicals	1.3
		agricultural products and foodstuffs	0.7
		total (including others)	5.5

source: *The Economist*, 2002

MAIN TRADING PARTNERS

EXPORTS

IMPORTS

%		%	
46.1	USA	10.9	USA
10.7	India	9.2	France
6.1	Spain	8.7	Germany
3.4	France	7.4	UK
33.7	others	63.8	others

source: *CIA World Factbook*, 2002

Flaring tempers

Natural gas is often found where people drill for oil. For many years, it has been burnt off as a by-product. Gas flares on oil rigs shoot burning jets of gas 24 hours a day in some parts of the delta, and some have been doing so for more than 40 years.

Local people complain that the gas flares damage the environment, pollute the air and cause sickness and ill health. Flaring has been linked to acid rain, which stunts crops and poisons drinking water as well as rivers, **mangrove** swamps and wildlife. People living near these flares are deprived of the night's natural darkness. Also, people are unhappy with the waste of this natural resource.

Nigeria has the largest natural gas reserves in Africa – some say the world. Only a fraction of the gas is currently used. Today, people are investigating ways to make money from natural gas as well as how it can benefit local communities. A small proportion is refined and bottled and sold within Nigeria as liquid gas fuel. Since 1984, oil companies have had to inject a proportion of this gas back into the Earth. The companies also have to pay a fine to the Nigerian government for every barrel of gas they burn. However, companies continue to practise flaring in the delta because it is the cheapest way to get rid of the gas, even with the fines.

Cacao and rubber are the only other significant exports. Imports include machinery, transport equipment, spare parts, iron and steel products, textiles, paper products, chemicals and food. Most imports come from European countries or the USA.

INDUSTRY

Nigeria's industry is dominated by mining, especially the drilling of oil. The oil business is the most important and fastest growing sector. After mining, manufacturing is growing fastest.

Mining

Nigeria's most valuable mineral resources are crude oil, natural gas (see box on page 85), coal, tin and columbite (a black mineral that contains iron).

A band of coal deposits stretches across the country from Benin to Cameroon. Once the vastly more profitable and more plentiful oil deposits were discovered, however, coal mining declined, although it has since been revived. Coal is still used by the railways and metalworkers, and to generate electricity.

Corruption and resistance

For decades of military rule, and particularly under General Sani Abacha, the leaders of Nigeria skimmed billions of pounds from the oil industry. Without democratic elections, Nigerians were powerless to stop this plundering of their chief natural resource. If anyone campaigned to see more direct benefits from the hugely profitable oil industry, they were in danger of being arrested and thrown in jail, or worse. Ken Saro-Wiwa was one such activist and a member of the Movement for the Survival of the Ogoni People (MOSOP). In the early 1990s, tens of thousands of people joined MOSOP to oppose the devastation their homeland was suffering at the hands of the oil industry. General Sani Abachi unleashed the military, who brutalized the delta's people. Hundreds were tortured and imprisoned. Ken Saro-Wiwa and eight other activists were hanged by the dictatorship in 1995, despite international outrage.

MAJOR INDUSTRIES

The area around the former capital, Lagos, is the most heavily industrialized region in Nigeria. Drilling for oil takes place in the delta region, both onshore and offshore. Most mining occurs on the Jos Plateau.

Tin and columbite are mined largely on the Jos Plateau. The demand for tin and columbite has decreased since the 1980s, however. Iron-ore deposits in Kwara state have been mined since 1984. A plant processes the ore and supplies the iron to the steel complex at nearby Ajaokuta. Limestone is widespread in Nigeria. This chalky rock is used in the steel industry and to make cement. Small amounts of gold, sapphires, copper and talc are also mined.

The oil boom

In 1956, oil was discovered in the delta, and Nigeria's oil industry was born. Later, more reserves were discovered in deep-water deposits offshore, where drilling is increasingly being done. Booming oil prices since the 1970s led to rapid economic growth, and today, the government gets most of its money from the oil industry. Factories, roads, railways, bridges and government services have all been funded by the oil business.

Little of Nigeria's oil is sold as anything other than crude oil or crude petroleum. Outside the country,

An oil spill from a pipeline devastated parts of the delta inhabited by Ijaw people in 2001, killing fish stocks and damaging the environment. Delta people complain that the oil companies do not do enough to compensate them when such spills occur.

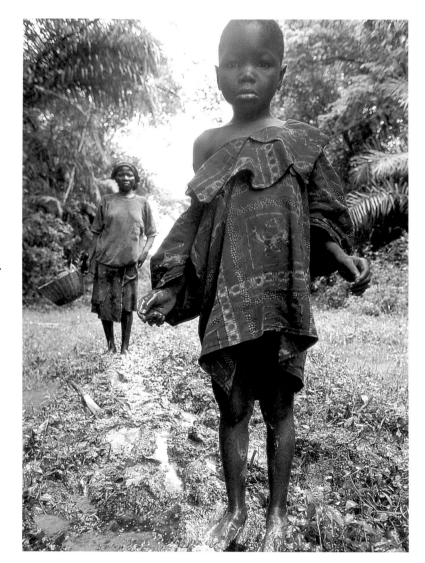

foreign (non-Nigerian) companies use the crude oil or petroleum to make a range of more profitable products, from refined petroleum to margarine and paints. Oil refineries at Port Harcourt, Warri, Abuja and Kaduna in Nigeria turn crude oil into crude or refined petroleum.

Oil spills

Oil spills are a sensitive topic in Nigeria. Delta people complain that the oil companies neither maintain pipes adequately nor clean up properly after the numerous oil spills that occur every year. Oil companies accuse Nigerians of deliberately sabotaging pipelines. Sabotage does sometimes happen, when people attempt to siphon off oil from overland pipes, for instance.

Under Nigerian law, companies do not have to clean up or compensate for the effects of spills caused by sabotage. Communities complain that while sabotage claims are common, they are rarely proved in court. Nevertheless, some oil companies, including Shell, have made promises to lay all pipelines underground.

Whatever their origin, both large and small oil spills pollute the delta. Oil slicks poison drinking water, destroy crops and farmland, and kill fish and other wildlife. People with little money and no alternative are forced to drink polluted water, causing ill health.

The price of oil has swung up and down markedly since the 1980s, which has made it difficult for the government to invest in health, education and welfare projects consistently.

Manufacturing

A great deal of manufacturing goes on in Nigeria. People build their own homes, and make their own clothes and farming tools and even the dishes they eat off. Items might be made to sell at the local market or to trade with neighbours. Such small-scale production makes up the bulk of manufacturing in Nigeria.

Money earned from the oil industry has allowed the government to build large-scale manufacturing businesses, such as the steel mills at Ajaokuta and Aladja and pulp and paper mills at Oku Iboku and Iwopin. The steel and pulp and paper mills were set up in remote rural areas. New towns have sprung up around these industries, supplying workers and services to the mills. Smaller and often privately owned factories produce textiles, palm oil, cement, cigarettes, fertilizer, footwear, jewellery and drinks. Most factories are in and around the Lagos area or near other state capitals.

In the past, the Nigerian government took some measures to give Nigerians more control and ownership of factories and businesses. However, many are still managed and controlled by multinational companies.

ENERGY
SOURCES

%

64 oil, gas, coal & diesel

36 hydroelectricity

source: *CIA World Factbook*, 2002

The Oshogbo Dam stands on the Oshun River in Oyo state. Nigeria generates more than a third of its energy through hydroelectricity.

The most powerful multinationals in Nigeria are oil companies. Shell accounts for more than 40 per cent of the volume of oil production in Nigeria. ExxonMobil and ChevronTexaco produce much of the remainder. Other companies in the delta are the Italian company Agip and France's Elf-Aquitaine (or Elf). The Nigerian government has managed to 'Nigerianize' these companies to some extent. All of them work as joint ventures with the Nigerian government, which has 55 to 60 per cent interest in their operations.

Power to the people

Demand for electricity is greater than the supply in Nigeria. For the majority, wood is still the most important energy source. It is used to cook food and heat water in most homes, even in urban areas. Experts are worried that Nigeria could run out of wood, however, if present rates of tree logging continue.

Of the electricity that Nigeria produces itself, more than one-third is generated by hydroelectric power stations. The main sources of hydroelectric power are the Kainji, Shiroro and Jebba dams. With more invest-ment, hydroelectricity has the potential to meet even more of Nigeria's power needs. Meanwhile, much of Nigeria's electricity is produced at stations powered by fossil fuels such as coal and natural gas. There are fossil-fuel power stations at Igbin, Afam, Sapele and Lagos.

TRANSPORTATION

Cars are the most important means of transportation in Nigeria. Nigeria's road network follows a general north to south pattern established during the colonial era. More recent additions link the east and west. Dense networks of all-weather roads crosshatch south-western and south-eastern Nigeria, the Jos Plateau tin fields and the Kano–Katsina region. Elsewhere, and in the Cross River region, roads are fewer and more likely

Buses and vans wait to pick up passengers in Oshodi market in Lagos. The large number of vehicles on the road in the cities sometimes causes huge gridlocks, or 'go slows', to develop, slowing traffic to a standstill.

to be unpaved. An uncertain economy has halted the upkeep of roads in places. In Lagos, the huge numbers of vehicles and pedestrians on the roads have slowed journeys. Gridlocks known as 'go slows' jam roads with pedestrians and cars.

Cars are too expensive for many Nigerians to buy and keep on the road for their own personal use. To get around more cheaply, people share taxis or lorries. 'Bush taxis' take several passengers at a time, each one paying part of the fare. For single passengers, motorcycle taxis are an equally affordable way to get around cities. Privately owned minibuses run unofficial bus services, with each passenger paying a set fare. Buses link the major cities.

Railways link the north and south, from Lagos to Kano, and from Port Harcourt to Kano and Maiduguri. Trains mostly carry passengers, not freight.

TRANSPORTATION

The railway network in Nigeria connects Lagos and Port Harcourt, in the south, with Kaduna and Kano, in the north, and Maiduguri, in the east. Steam engines were used until the 1960s, when they were replaced by diesel. About one-third of the roads in Nigeria are paved and are passable in all weathers.

Communications

Nigeria has one of the best telephone networks in Africa. A satellite system links all the major towns and cities. Radio broadcasts from more than 60 Nigerian stations reach most of the country. There are television broadcasts in urban areas, but few rural areas can receive television signals. The National Television Station, NTA, is federally owned. Thirty states have their own television stations, and there are nine privately owned television stations and two private satellite television services. The majority of broadcasts are Nigerian productions, often in regional languages. The Press Law of 1993 limits foreign programmes broadcast by local TV stations to 40% of broadcasting time.

By air

Nigeria has a well-developed air transportation system. Nigeria Airways competes with several private airlines. Most state capitals have a national airport, and there are international airports at Lagos, Port Harcourt, Abuja and Kano. Lagos and Kano are the busiest airports. Only Lagos and Port Harcourt receive planes from other west African countries, and Kano gets a lot of traffic from north Africa. Helicopters ferry oil industry workers around the delta and Port Harcourt.

By water

Rivers have transported people and goods around Nigeria for a long time. The delta has relatively few roads, and canoeing the network of creeks and channels is still the most important way of getting about for many people. Motorboats, rowboats and ferries link coastal islands with the mainland. The Niger and Benue rivers carry large amounts of goods across the country. During the rainy season, boats on the Benue can travel far into Cameroon.

Lagos and Port Harcourt are the most important international seaports. Bonny, near Port Harcourt, and Burutu, near Warri, export the most crude oil. Warri, Sapele, Koko and Calabar are smaller regional ports.

Arts and living

'Diversity is not an abnormality but the very reality of our planet.'

Chinua Achebe, Nigerian novelist

Home to more than 250 different **ethnic groups,** Nigeria is a country of great cultural diversity. Generally speaking, each ethnic group has its own history and language. At certain times in the past, members of some ethnic groups followed the same religion and way of life, and produced similar artworks. Ethnicity is a very complex issue, however. It is easy to assume that the members of an ethnic group all live and behave in certain ways because of centuries of tradition. Yet people and society change and have done throughout history. As more and more people are educated, move to cities, listen to the radio and watch television, this process of change continues.

ARTS

Nigeria has a rich art history that includes sculpture, carving, metalwork, architecture and weaving. Equally popular and widespread art forms include performances by masked dancers and storytellers. There is a growing international and home market for Nigeria's art, both historic and modern.

Nigerian art is sometimes called ethnic art, which suggests there are recognizable ethnic styles. Although that is sometimes true, it is not always possible to figure out which ethnic group an artist belongs to just by studying his or her work. Yoruba artists work in a

An official in traditional dress parades on horseback during the Durbah Salah, a festival held in honour of the emir at Katsina in northern Nigeria.

variety of styles, for example. Artists and craftworkers adapt and develop styles as they work. The names of carvers of particular skill and creativity are remembered for generations, especially among the Yoruba.

Multipurpose art

As well as being pleasing or interesting to look at, Nigerian art often has other, sometimes more important, purposes. Among the Yoruba, for example, chiefs and kings commissioned carved wooden doors and house posts to make their homes or palaces more impressive. A great deal of historic Benin art was made for the *oba*'s (king's) court. Court art asserts the authority of the ruler, since it was made only for the *oba*. In Benin, the *oba*'s wealth, which court art represents, was believed to be linked to that of his kingdom.

The famous brass wall plaques from Benin's palace depict key events and people. Cast metal or carved wooden heads were either trophies or commemorative. Trophy heads depict slain enemies; commemorative heads are reminders of ancestors or past rulers. Either type might have an elaborately carved ivory tusk attached to the top, but it is not always clear whether a head is a trophy or commemorative.

Religious art

A great deal of Nigerian art has a religious or social purpose. In the south, carved wooden figures on altars often represent gods, spirits or ancestors. Shrines sculpted from mud are decorated with wooden, clay or cement figures up to life size. Chalk designers decorate the walls and floor of the shrines. Such shrines are often made and decorated by women.

Yoruba mothers who have lost a twin child might carry a small wooden *ibeji* (twin) figure. The mother may feed and wash the doll, showing her care for the child even after it has passed over to the spirit world. Some women may also carry *ibeji* while their twins are alive.

In the past certain arts were generally done by men, and others typically by women. Weaving and pottery were often the business of women, while wood carving was mostly done by men. Until recently only men were allowed to cast metal in Benin.

Popular locations for sculptures include roadside shrines, like this one in eastern Nigeria. The figures in the shrines represent gods, spirits, or ancestors.

Contemporary art

In 1914, the *oba* of Benin allowed court art to be sold to outsiders. This allowed metalworking, weaving and carving to flourish, and a wider Nigerian art market to emerge. In the 1940s, a palace carver continued the tradition that began with the plaque makers by creating a series of clay and cement reliefs. Cement sculpture is now a popular art form in Edo state. Life-size cement figures grace ancestral altars and many public places. Working in the Yoruba tradition, modern artists carve wooden doors for hospitals, churches, businesses and government offices. Instead of chiefs and *obas*, the door panels depict scenes from modern life, such as patients in a surgery or a busy office.

Spinning silk and weaving cloth

Nigeria is well known for its variety of textiles, including embroidery, weaving, **adire** (shown here) and silk-screen printing. Many of the fabrics were woven by women on vertical looms. Since the 1950s, however, hand weaving has declined in Nigeria. It is slow and demanding work, and women now have more career opportunities. Artificial **indigo** and brightly coloured imported fabrics have largely replaced *adire* and hand-dyed indigo cloth in many parts.

In the past, Yoruba and Nupe weavers span silk from the cocoons of local silk moths. The pale beige silk was made into robes for kings, chiefs and wealthy men.

Since the 1900s, however, imported and artificial silks have turned silk spinning into a lost art.

For many decades, dyes made from indigo plants have been used throughout west Africa to dye white cloth a dark blue. Before Yoruba *adire* cloth is dyed indigo, patterns are marked on the fabric in wax or starch, which resist dyeing. Alternatively, patterns are stitched, tied or folded into the cloth before it is dyed. *Adire* is used to make everyday clothes, unlike **aso oke** cloth, which Yoruba people often keep as a family heirloom. Today, weavers might use lurex thread to add a sheen to *adire* cloth.

In some areas, houses made of clay are often decorated with relief designs, such as this house in Zaria.

Nigeria has also produced some internationally famous modern artists, including painter and etcher Twins Seven Seven (born 1945). In the 1960s, Twins' illustrations of spirit figures from Nigerian literature and folklore first attracted world attention. Twins now lives in the USA, and his art hangs in museums and galleries around the world.

Architecture

Buildings in cities and towns are often made of modern materials such as concrete, cement or brick. In rural areas or the older parts of towns, however, many people still live in buildings made of clay, stone or wood.

Hausa people often build with pear-shaped bricks of clay that are dried in the sun. The walls are plastered with more clay. Around Nok, the Jaba people are famous for their oval houses almost sculpted from clay. Clay houses often have designs moulded or painted on their walls and, in rural areas, thatched roofs. China plates or colourful enamel bowls might be set into walls and ceilings. Some Nupe people set specially made terracotta saucers into their walls. Before the clay wall dries, the saucer is shattered to create mosaic-like patterns.

Beating and casting

Metal has to be either beaten or melted and poured into shape. Nigerian metalworkers use both techniques. Some metalwokers beat sheets of iron into flattened, bent, twisted or tube-like shapes to make a Yoruba priest's staff. More commonly, metalworkers use the lost-wax process. In this process, an exact model of the item to be cast is made in wax, or sometimes in latex tapped from the rubber tree. The model is covered in layers of clay. After the clay has dried, the whole thing is heated until the wax melts. The molten wax is poured out of a hole in the clay mould. Latex does not melt but is burnt to a fine ash instead. This leaves an empty space the exact shape of the wax model. Molten metal is then poured into the clay mould and left to harden. When the clay is removed, a metal copy of the wax model is left. The advantage of this ancient technique is that detailed shapes made in easy-to-work soft wax can be copied in hard-wearing metal.

Art in the Muslim north

The **Islamic** societies in northern Nigeria have rich art histories. Artistic creativity is expressed in a variety of ways in northern Nigeria, from architecture and house murals to dyeing and leatherwork.

In Kano, masters of ancient dyeing techniques create what many consider to be works of art on fabric. Designs are folded into the fabric before it is dyed. The dye cannot penetrate the folds, and patterns are created. The Hausa have long been famous makers of **indigo** cloth.

Northern craftworkers, especially the Hausa, are also famous for their skilled leatherwork. Saddles, bags and other items are richly decorated with stitching and appliqué, in which sewn-on shapes create patterns.

Hausa architects and craftworkers have decorated the inside walls of houses with moulded and painted designs for many generations. Since the 20th century, outside walls have also become canvasses for this art form. Walls are often covered with complex, inter-locking patterns of lines and shapes. Or modern motifs such as images of bicycles, cars or even computers might be moulded on to walls. Hausa architects are also famous for larger-scale public works. The Friday Mosque in Zaria was built in the 19th century by famed Hausa architect Babba Gwani for the **emir**. The roof is supported by a vaulting system of arched palm trunks plastered with mud.

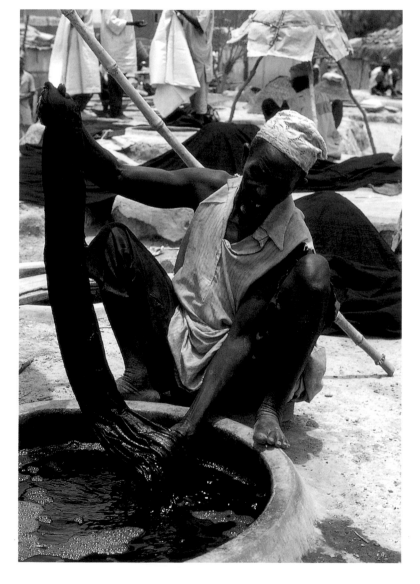

This man is dyeing fabric in Kano's indigo dye pits, in much the same way that people have for generations. The pits are thought to be among the oldest in Africa.

Making masks

Africa is famous for its masks. In particular, many Nigerian peoples have a history of making masks, including the Yoruba, Igbo, delta peoples and the **Muslim** Nupe. In Nigeria, masked dancers wearing colourful or fearsome costumes are accompanied by drummers, dancers, musicians and singers at street events called masquerades.

In the past, nearly every Nigerian town and village held some sort of masquerade. Masquerades were staged for a range of reasons – to bring a good harvest, warn wrongdoers to behave well, show respect for rulers or ancestors or to celebrate the initiation of young men or women into adulthood. During the colonial era, maskers would take the opportunity to mock their European rulers and their habits, a practice that has continued to the present day. Each April, masqueraders

During Yoruba ancestor-worship festivals, called egungun, masqueraders wear masks and costumes that conceal their whole body apart from the feet.

From Nigeria, to South America, to London

The world's biggest street carnivals have their roots in west African masquerades, perhaps even Nigerian ones. The Eyo festival in Lagos claims to be the direct ancestor of the modern-day carnival in Brazil. When Africans were enslaved and taken across the Atlantic to the Americas (see pages 64–5), they took their religions and cultures with them. In the New World, many were forbidden from practising their own faiths by white slave owners, but Africans continued to masquerade. Few whites understood that these events had any religious or social roles. If masquerades adopted Christian symbols or were held on saint's days, they were even less likely to be disrupted. Over many generations, these public performances evolved into huge street carnivals, especially in Rio de Janeiro, in Brazil, and Trinidad, in the Caribbean. Notting Hill Carnival in London was founded by Caribbean immigrants to the UK in the 1960s. That carnival, too, is a descendant of west African masquerades, via the Americas.

perform at Yoruba ancestor festivals (*egungun*). *Gelede* masquerades were originally intended to keep the peace with female witches, whom the masked dancers sought to entertain. In a roundabout way, *gelede* dancers showed respect for the powers of women.

Today, masquerades are increasingly held to entertain the public and tourists or to mark the visit of an important person. The Eyo festival in Lagos, for example, is held whenever tradition or occasion demands. It might be part of the funeral of an *oba* of Lagos or held to honour an important visitor.

At important festivals and events in the south-east, especially among the Igbo people of Anambra state, *atilogwu* dancers often perform. '*Atilogwu*' means 'is this magic?' in Igbo. Dressed in brilliantly coloured costumes, *atilogwu* dancers are highly trained and dance to foot-stomping rhythms. The young men and women dancers astound onlookers with their skilful gymnastics. Troupes of dancers have performed around the world, and *atilogwu* has become an international symbol of Nigerian culture.

Music

Nigeria is one of Africa's musical centres, and has been for a long time. Praise singers and court musicians – including drummers, trumpeters and rattle and bell players – among the Hausa, Edo and Yoruba have been performing at palaces and chiefs' dwellings for hundreds of years. Today, famous praise singers can earn hundreds of pounds a night singing the praises of notable or wealthy people, such as politicians, at weddings, festivals and ceremonies. Hausa court singers still perform for emirs and other royalty at private functions. A new twist on this tradition is the singing of songs of abuse at political rallies.

Modern music

The modern music scene in Nigeria is one of the largest in Africa, and Lagos is at its heart. There are many Nigerian recording studios, record labels and pressing plants making vinyl records. With a huge home market, there is enough demand for music to support artists who sing in regional languages.

Before the 1920s, **palm-wine music** grew up in the drinking establishments men gathered in after work. Singers elaborated on current issues and used proverbs to illustrate their points. They were backed by stringed instruments and makeshift shakers and **calabash** rattles.

In the 1960s, a uniquely Nigerian form of breezy and brassy **highlife** music – a type of dance band music – was the fashion. With the introduction of amplified sound, **juju** – a variation of palm-wine music – became a popular urban dance music, and it has been one of the most popular music styles in Nigeria since the 1970s, eclipsing highlife.

Fuji has swept other styles off Lagos dance floors in the 1990s. Described as a wall of percussion, fuji is based on Yoruba drumming and percussion but rarely uses stringed instruments. Both juju and fuji are sung in local languages, especially Yoruba.

The first juju musicians were palm-wine singers. I.K. Dairo and King Sunny Ade are international stars and the most famous juju musicians.

Radical Afro-beats

One of Africa's most radical and challenging musicians, Fela Anikulapo Ransome Kuti (1938–97), was born in Abeokuta, Nigeria. His grandfather was a composer and his father was a pianist. Fela studied music in London and met members of the Black Panthers civil rights group in the USA during the 1960s, which helped form his ideas and strong desire for change.

Fela was solely responsible for **Afro-beat**. Influenced by African soul music, he mixed elements of highlife and jazz music and used traditional and modern instruments. Twenty-strong backing choruses sang in a call-and-response style. On stage, Fela switched between saxophone, alto sax and keyboard. He brought his forceful personality and passionate music to bear on military rule, poverty, unfair arrest, traffic and even skin bleaching. His defiant lyrical attacks on military rulers were a rallying call for the Nigerian poor and activists and political prisoners worldwide. Sung in pidgin English, the songs gained him a huge following. Since his death, the following of his son Femi Kuti has grown.

Musical instruments

Hausa musicians play a long court trumpet called *kakakai*. The *kakakai* is accompanied by drums, of which they are several hundred types. Throughout Nigeria, virtuoso drummers on talking drums mimic the effects of tonal languages, such as Yoruba and Igbo. The drums beat out proverbs, praise poems and relate histories. Stringed instruments include the Hausa's one-string fiddle (*goje*) and the Igbo's thirteen-string *obo*.

Literature

Wole Soyinka was the first black African to win a Nobel Prize for literature, in 1986. Born in Abeokuta, he was an outspoken critic of Nigeria's military rulers.

Nigeria has more published novelists, poets and playwrights than any other west African country. Many have been read and enjoyed around the world. This huge body of published works is dwarfed by another type of literature in Nigeria – oral literature, which is spoken rather than written. It includes praise songs, epic poems, proverbs, myths and legends, poetry and songs. The Yoruba alone have several types of sung

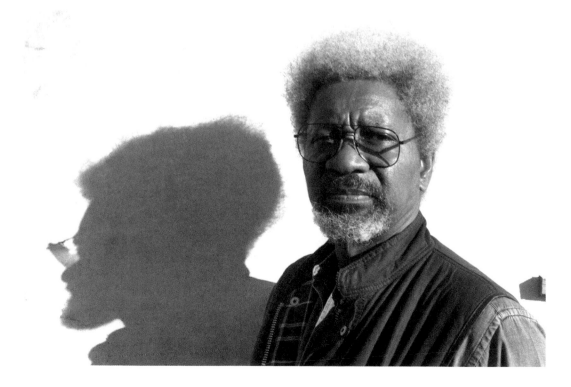

poetry, including hunter's songs (*ijala*), town and family histories (*orile*) and masker's poems (*iwi*). Epic poems are long, complicated stories on a grand scale, with casts of many and plots that span hundreds of years. There are epic poems about most of the states that existed before Nigeria did. Professional storytellers are paid to sing or recite at celebrations and other events.

Writing and writers

The history of Nigeria's written literature began more than 200 years ago, with Olaudah Equiano's slave narrative (see box on page 66), although Nigeria did not exist when Equiano's book was published in 1789. Since then, hundreds of writers have earned fame at home, and almost as many are known around the world.

Amos Tutuola (1920–97) was the first Nigerian writer to win international fame. Tutuola's *The Palm-Wine Drinkard* [sic] (1952) is a mythical tale that is rambling and poetic with a grim humour.

Chinua Achebe's 1950s books about the impact of Western culture on Nigerian society still appear on the reading lists of English literature students today. *Things Fall Apart* (1958) delicately but compellingly follows the effects of British rule on an Igbo village. Since independence, Achebe has continued to write about the effects of poor rule and bad rulers on Nigerian people.

In 1986, Wole Soyinka (born 1934) became the first black African to win a Nobel Prize for literature. Many of Soyinka's thoughtful but at times tragic plays, novels and poems, as well as non-fiction, dwell on what it means to be a Nigerian, or an African, today.

Many women have written about similar themes. Buchi Emecheta (born 1944) has brought to life the experiences of Nigerian women at home and in the UK in books such as *In the Ditch* (1972), *The Joys of Motherhood* (1979) and *Kehinde* (1994).

In 1991, Ben Okri (born 1959) won the Booker Prize with *The Famished Road*. In a part-real, part-magical

Oral literatures act like history books. They relate the history of a nation, ethnic group, ruler or family, keeping it alive for future generations.

style, the book depicts the life of an *abiku* (spirit child). *Abiku* are spirits born only to die soon after, since they long for the spirit world. Okri's hero decides to stay, and the child's struggles reflect Nigeria's struggles.

Among Nigeria's, and Africa's, published poets, Christopher Okigbo (1932–67) and John Pepper Clark-Bekederemo (born 1935) are probably the best known. Okigbo's carefully crafted poems are dense with meaning, while Clark's are more urgent and lyrical. Through his poetry, Okigbo tried to convey his visions for a better Nigeria. An Igbo, he was killed during the Biafran War (see box on page 72).

EVERYDAY LIFE

In cities and towns, people's daily life is similar to urban dwellers everywhere. Yet life can be hard in a Nigerian city. There are not enough jobs to go around, so many people create their own job opportunities – there is no social security system to rely on. To earn money, a person might try trading, craftwork, soap-making, driving a taxi, guiding tourists or selling street snacks. In poorer parts of town, housing is also in short supply.

Outside of towns and cities, daily life is centred around farming, herding or fishing. At harvest time, villagers help their family and neighbours, knowing that the favour will be returned. As more people move to cities, however, farmers increasingly have to pay for such help. Many farmers also trade, work for wages out of the growing season or are craftworkers.

Family and home life

Most Nigerian families, especially in rural areas, live in compounds. A compound is made up of several linked houses, often organized around an open courtyard. Southern houses are more likely to be a single storey than northern ones. A typical Nigerian compound might be home to a husband, one or more wives, children and grandparents.

HOW NIGERIANS SPEND THEIR MONEY

%

- 53 food and drink
- 11.4 fuel and light
- 6 clothing and footwear
- 4.7 transportation
- 3.8 household goods
- 21.1 other

source: *Encyclopaedia Britannica*

Nigerian men are allowed to marry more than one wife each. In the Islamic north, the number is limited to four. The first wife tends to be the most senior and takes charge of newer wives. Each wife might have her own compound, or a husband might live with all his wives in one compound. Children mostly live with their mother. Women and men look after their own money, so both are financially independent. As Nigerian society changes, however, marriage patterns also change. More and more women no longer share, or want to share, their husband with other wives.

Food and drink

Most southern meals are based around root crops such as cassava and yams, or rice. Cassava flour (*gari*) is used to make porridge (*eba*). *Gari* is fermented and pounded to make *fufu*. Yams are ground then boiled to make *àmàlà*. In the south, they are also pounded after boiling

Fish stew is a popular item on the menu in many street markets. Dried fish, usually cod, is imported, while seafood from the coastal regions is transported across the country.

Pepper soup

This southern recipe is made with palm oil, but vegetable oil can be used instead.

You will need:

500 g (1 lb) meat, chicken or fish

2 diced onions

water

4 stock cubes

salt

3–4 fresh tomatoes

1–2 green peppers

a little palm oil or vegetable oil

ground black pepper

Method:

Put the meat and onion in a pan with a small amount of water. Add the stock cubes and a pinch of salt and cook until the meat is almost tender. Mash the tomatoes and the peppers together with the oil and pour the blended mixture into the pan. Cook for about 20–30 minutes, stirring constantly. Add salt and pepper.

to make a light but thick and shiny paste that is usually eaten with a sauce based on palm oil or peanuts.

Dishes based around grains such as sorghum or rice dominate the northern diet. *Tuwo da miya* is a thick sorghum porridge eaten with a spicy, vegetable-based sauce.

Accompaniments are meat and vegetable soups, stews, sauces and omelette-like dishes. *Jollof* rice is a dish made of rice cooked with palm oil and served with vegetables and meat. Stocks made from meat or fish flavour stews and thicken soups. Salty, dried fish, which are often imported, are popular. Meats eaten are either beef, goat, chicken, mutton or lamb. Camel kebabs are eaten in the north, though ones made of beef or mutton are more common. People eat pork in the south but not in the Muslim north (Muslims do not eat pork). In cities and the countryside, people also eat bushmeat (any wild animal caught for food), including antelope and giant rodents called cane rats or grass cutters.

Vegetables such as banana-like plantain, spinach-like bitter leaf and pumpkin leaves are often fried. Slices of fried plantain taste like slightly sweet potato chips. Okra is used as a thickener. Fritters of black-eyed beans and fried bean cakes are among the drier dishes. More unusual delicacies include *igbin* – large forest snails – which are served with an extremely hot sauce.

Education

In the past, some societies in Nigeria provided formal instruction as part of young people's initiation into adulthood. In some places, young people are still initiated into adulthood in this way, but the practice is declining. In Islamic communities, many children, especially boys, attend schools where they study the Qur'an, the Muslim holy book, in the evenings or at weekends as well as attending day school. Fewer girls than boys go to school at all levels, partly because parents, particularly in the north, prefer to have the help of girls at home.

The government partly or wholly funds primary education all over the country, and the federal government runs secondary schools called unity schools in all states. There are also many privately owned schools as well as technical colleges, polytechnics and universities.

Nigerian children start school at the age of six and spend six years at primary school. Some also spend six years at secondary school. The majority of children attend primary school, but only a minority go on to secondary education and even fewer go to higher education.

These pupils are at St Michael's School in Ibiade, Osun state, a school that is supported by Voluntary Service Overseas (VSO). International aid projects help communities build their own schools in some places.

EDUCATIONAL ATTENDANCE

university and college	4%
secondary school	33%
primary school	98%

source: *The Economist*, 2002

About 68 per cent of adult Nigerians are literate (can read and write), compared with an average of 71 per cent for developing countries. Only 61 per cent of Nigerian women are literate, compared with about 76 per cent of men.

Health care

Lack of funding has left Nigeria with poor health-care facilities. From 1994 to 1997, government health spending averaged just 4.5 per cent of the budget. Nigerians are still more likely to die from preventable or curable diseases than people in other developing countries. Often, the diseases are related to poverty. Diarrhoea, respiratory infections and malaria are made worse by poor access to clean water. Nigeria does have a high number of doctors and nurses relative to the size of the population, however.

Nigeria's health-care system also suffers from 'brain drain': the loss of skilled professionals to other countries. In 1995, the ministry of health estimated that 21,000 Nigerian doctors were practising in the USA alone, roughly the same number that were working in Nigeria. Low pay, military rule and poor facilities have driven many health workers away.

Despite all these problems, the government has carried out important health-care programmes, such as childhood immunization and treatment for diarrhoea. It has also funded community health-care programmes to try to improve people's access to basic health care and to provide information on diseases such as AIDS.

Religion

The majority of people in the north are Muslim, while those in the south are more likely to be Christian. Christians are either Catholic, Protestant or members of one of Nigeria's many independent churches, such as the Yoruba-based Cherubim and Seraphim. Independent churches often incorporate African cultural practices such as drumming, dancing and faith healing. Many people keep aspects of their African religion alive while belonging to a church. Igbo Christians, for example, might attend church as well as maintain a shrine to their *chi* (personal god). Many Christians keep shrines or altars dedicated to their ancestors.

How to say ...

Yoruba is a group of closely related languages, not one language. Yoruba and Igbo are tonal languages. A rise or fall in pitch (tone) affects a word's meaning. For example, a simple Yoruba word such as 'igba' can mean 'time', 'two hundred', 'halved calabash' or 'locust tree', depending on the speaker's tone. (Tone is not included in the pronunciations below.) Hausa is widely spoken throughout west Africa. It has been used as a trading language for several hundred years. Before the 1900s, Hausa was written in Arabic. Today, it is more often written in Roman script, like English.

Yoruba numbers

One *Eni* (eh-nee)

Two *Eji* (eh-jee)

Three *Eta* (eh-ta-ah)

Four *Erin* (hey-reen)

Five *Erun* or *Arun* (eh-roon *or* ah-roon)

Six *Efa* (eh-faah)

Seven *Eje* (eh-jay)

Eight *Ejo* (eh-joor *or* eh-joh)

Nine *Esan* (eh-saan)

Ten *Ewa* (eh-waah)

Igbo greetings and phrases

Good day *Ezigbo ubosi* (ah-zeh-Boh oo-bee-oh-see; 'B' stands for a very hard 'b' sound written as 'gb')

How are you? *Kedu* (key-ah-dee-oo)

I am fine *Odi mma* (oh-dee mme-ahh)

Thank you *Dalu* (dee-ahh-lee-oh)

Yes *Eyi* or *ehe* (ah-ye-eh or ah-he-ah)

No *Mba* (me-bee-ahh)

Igbo numbers

One *Ofu* (oh-fee-oo)

Two *Abua* (ahh-bee-oo-ahh)

Three *Ato* (ahh-tea-uh)

Four *Ano* (ahh-nee-oh)

Five *Ise* (eh-see-ah)

Six *Isii* (eh-see-eh-eh)

Seven *Asaa* (ahh-see-ahh-ahh)

Eight *Asato* (ahh-see-ahh-tea-oh)

Nine *Itenani* (eh-tea-nee-ahh-nee-ni)

Ten *Ili* (eh-lee-eh)

Hausa greetings and phrases

Hello *Sannu* (sa-noo)

Response to 'hello' *Sannu kadai* (sa-noo kah-die)

Please *Don Allah* (don ah-lah)

Thank you *Na gode* (nah gode)

Yes *I* (ee)

No *A'a* (ah uh)

Hausa numbers

One *Daya* (day-ah)

Two *Biyu* (bee-yoo)

Three *Uku* (oo-koo)

Four *Hudu* (hoo-doo)

Five *Biyar* (bee-yar)

Six *Shida* (shee-dah)

Seven *Bokwai* (bok-why)

Eight *Takwas* (tak-was)

Nine *Tara* (tah-rah)

Ten *Goma* (goh-mah)

Festivals and public holidays

1 January: New Year's Day; Ekpe – three-day harvest festival in the Niger Delta
February–March, every other year: Pategi Regatta at an important crossing point of the Niger south of Jebba; Argungu fishing festival, near Sokoto
Usually April: Egungun – Yoruba ancestor-worship festivals, with masquerades and sporting events; Ikeji Izuogu – a yam festival in Imo state
1 May: May Day, or Workers' Day
June to August: festivals in numerous towns in honour of Yoruba god Ogun
August/September: festival in Osogbo in honour of Yoruba river goddess Osun
1 October: Independence Day; Sekiapu – masquerades and river events in River and Cross River states
December: Igue – procession of the *oba* of Benin; Ofala – Ontisha festival in honour of traditional ruler, who appears before his people
25 December: Christmas Day

Muslim festivals
Muslim festivals follow the lunar calendar, which is based on the phases of the Moon, so they occur at different times each year. The main ones are:
Ramadan – a month of fasting during daylight hours
Eid el Fitr/Sallah – public holiday marking the end of Ramadan
Eid el Kabir/Tabaski – public holiday marking the time the prophet Abraham sacrificed a ram instead of his son
Muhammad's birthday/Mouloud – public holiday

African religions continue to thrive in Nigeria – in particular, the Yoruba religion. The creator god Olodumare (or Olorun) coexists with hundreds of *orisas* (gods), spirits and the ancestors of living Nigerians.

Some Muslim Hausa women have kept aspects of the pre-Islamic religion alive in the Bori cult. Although women do not usually go alone to public places in northern Muslim communities, members attend public meetings where they might be possessed by *bori* (spirits). Bori ceremonies allow women to meet up and find explanations and remedies for family problems such as divorce.

A sporting nation

Before the colonial era, wrestling was Nigeria's most popular sport. The British introduced football, boxing,

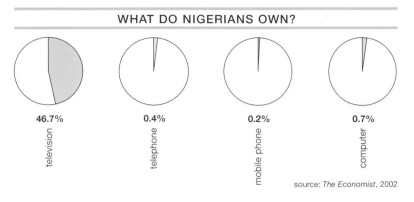

WHAT DO NIGERIANS OWN?

46.7% television

0.4% telephone

0.2% mobile phone

0.7% computer

source: *The Economist*, 2002

Almost half the households in Nigeria own a television set. Unlike people in Western countries, however, few people can afford to own a telephone or a computer.

athletics, cricket and table and lawn tennis. Today, football, boxing and athletics are the most popular sports in Nigeria, while basketball is gaining in popularity.

Huge crowds attend football matches in larger cities. The Super Eagles is Nigeria's national team. It has done well in the World Cup and won or been placed second in the Cup of African Nations several times. Several Nigerian star players are members of world-class European teams. The Nigeria's women's team won the African Championships in 1998.

The Nigerian national football team won the gold medal at the 1996 Atlanta Olympics in the USA. The team members are photographed here with their medals.

The future

*'This is just the beginning of a new dawn for our land ...
the day of our glory may indeed be a long one.'*

President Olesegun Obasanjo, 2003 presidential message

Nigeria faces many challenges now and in the future. Removing the military from politics and ensuring that democracy is kept in place are important to many Nigerians. However, perhaps the biggest challenge Nigeria faces – beating poverty – is the most complex, and a challenge that grows as the population increases.

Poverty creates many other problems, including crime, corruption, ill health, ethnic or regional conflict and environmental damage. In a vicious cycle, these problems hit the poor particularly badly, worsening their situation. Nigerians at all levels of society are trying to break this cycle.

Breaking the habit

One reason for the poverty in Nigeria is the country's dependence on oil. Nigeria's rulers borrowed a lot of money from the World Bank and its lending body, the International Monetary Fund (IMF), in the late 1970s and 1980s. Oil prices had fallen hard, leaving the government short of cash. At the same time, the cost of Nigeria's imports was greater than the revenue from its exports, creating a trade deficit. The borrowers were confident, however, that the price of oil would soon rise, correcting these problems. In fact, oil prices continued to fall, and by 2002, Nigeria owed a massive £21,334 million in foreign debt.

Street artists perform at a rally for Olesegun Obasanjo before he was elected president in 1999. Obasanjo was re-elected in 2003.

FACT FILE

● The year 2005 will be Nigeria's national year of tourism. Local governments have established tourist boards, and it will be easier to get tourist visas.

● Improving communications, energy and transport infrastructure, and increasing private investment in the non-oil sector, are the government's main economic challenges.

● Government and World Bank officials as well as charities, aid agencies, women's groups and community-based organizations are all focused on tackling poverty in Nigeria.

As a condition of aid, Nigeria adopted strict IMF economic policies in 1986. These involved cutting government spending, allowing more imports and loosening government control over business and trade.

Nigeria had great problems, however, meeting the debt repayments. The agreement with the IMF expired in 2001, and Nigeria received little aid in 2002. As a result, the government finds it hard to adequately fund school, health and environmental programmes. Meanwhile, to improve conditions within Nigeria, the civilian government is trying to break free from its dependency on oil. It has encouraged other sectors, such as agriculture, manufacturing and tourism, to develop.

Troubled times in the delta

The Niger Delta is one of the world's largest wetlands and home to many unique plants and animals. It is also where the country's oil reserves are found. The inhabitants of the delta have seen few benefits from the industrial activity in their communities, however, and the region is one of the poorest in Nigeria. There is electricity in only a few of the delta's towns, and fresh water and health-care facilities are poor.

Delta people hold the oil industry responsible for this situation, while the oil companies argue that developing the delta is the government's responsibility. Resentment has reached such levels that people have seized and destroyed oil-company property, as well as kidnapped or held oil workers hostage. Clashes in 2003 between protestors, police, army and oil workers around Warri resulted in the deaths of scores of people and the destruction of dozens of villages.

Oil companies and the government are beginning to listen, however. In 2000, a new law was passed that gives the nine oil-producing states 13 per cent of oil revenues. Before that, the states received just 3 per cent of oil revenues. Shell has set up pilot projects to develop new food crops and livestock. The government has set

In 2003, the US House of Representatives ordered Shell's Nigerian company to pay the Ijaw people of Bayelsa state £937 million to compensate them for hardship and environmental damage caused since 1956.

up the Niger Delta Development Committee, which encourages the involvement of the community and other interested parties in the region's development.

Ethnic and religious conflict

Any Nigerian government has the difficult task of respecting people's ethnic identity while ensuring that no one group is treated favourably or unfairly. This is a challenge in a country with hundreds of **ethnic groups** that are constantly changing and evolving.

Northerners often feel that southerners have been given more advantages – first, by the British and then, by the independent governments, who have generally been dominated by Yoruba and Igbo people. Debates about issues such as adopting Shari'a (**Islamic**) law have worsened relations between **Muslims** and Christians and have led to riots in which thousands of Nigerians have been killed, Muslim and Christian.

Women and development

For a long time, Nigeria's development plans neglected the roles of women as heads of households, traders, workers, educators and fee payers. The majority of food grown and eaten in Nigeria is farmed by women. More and more, however, officials and policy makers within Nigeria and at institutions such as the World Bank are recognizing that women are central to the success of development plans. Women have a say in family and household matters, the division and farming of land, the use of resources and the education of children. Women's groups have organized demonstrations and protests that have mobilized entire communities. For these reasons, women's voices are increasingly being listened to.

The challenges that Nigeria faces at the beginning of the 21st century are numerous and complex. With a wealth of natural resources, ambitious citizens and a new, civilian government, however, there is much hope among Nigerians that these challenges can be faced.

The government is planning to sell off (privatize) state-owned companies to private investors to increase government earnings and bring investment into Nigeria's underfunded industries. Not everyone agrees, however. Workers and trade unions fear job losses and higher prices will result.

Almanac

POLITICAL

country name:
official form: Federal Republic of Nigeria
short form: Nigeria

nationality:
noun: Nigerian(s)
adjective: Nigerian

official language: English

capital city: Abuja

type of government: republic

suffrage (voting rights):
everyone eighteen years and over

independence: 1 October 1960

national anthem: 'Arise O Compatriots'

national holiday:
1 October (Independence Day)

flag:

GEOGRAPHICAL

location: western Africa, bordering the North Atlantic Ocean, between Benin, to the west, and Cameroon, to the east

climate: equatorial in south, tropical in centre, arid in north

total area: 923, 768 sq km (356,667 sq miles)
land: 99%
water: 1%

coastline: 853 km (530 miles)

terrain: southern lowlands merge into central hills and plateaux; mountains in south-east, plains in north

highest point: Chappal Waddi 2419 m (7936 ft)

lowest point: Atlantic Ocean 0 m

land use (2001 est.):
arable land: 31%
permanent crops 2.6%
other uses: 66.4%

natural resources: petroleum, tin, columbite, iron ore, coal, limestone, lead, zinc, natural gas

natural hazards: periodic droughts

POPULATION

population (2000 UN est.): 111.6 million

population growth rate (2002 est.): 2.54%

birth rate (2002 est.): 39.2 births per 1000 of the population

death rate (2002 est.): 14.1 deaths per 1000 of the population

sex ratio (2002 est.): 103 males to 100 females

total fertility rate (2002 est.): 5.1 children born per woman

infant mortality rate (2002 est.): 72.5 deaths per 1000 live births

life expectancy at birth (2002 est.):
total population: 50.59 years
male: 50.58 years
female: 50.6 years

literacy:
total population: 68.5%
male: 76%
female: 61%

ECONOMY

currency: naira (N); 1 naira = 100 kobo

exchange rate (2003): £1 = N213

gross domestic product (2000): £25,687 million

average annual growth rate (1990–2000): 3.1%

GDP per capita (2000): £200

average annual inflation rate (1996–2000): 8.0%

unemployment rate (1997): 3.2%

exports (2000): £11,937 million

imports (2000): £5500 million

foreign debt (2002): £21,334 million

Human Development Index
(an index scaled from 0 to 100 combining statistics indicating adult literacy, years of schooling, life expectancy and income levels):

45.5 (UK 92.3)

TIMELINE—NIGERIA

World history

Nigerian history

c.50,000 BC

c.40,000
Modern humans –
*Homo sapiens
sapiens* – emerge

c.10,000
Humans settle
in Nigeria

c.3000 BC

3000–1000
Height of ancient
Egyptian
civilization

c.900 BC
Hunter-gathering
gives way to
subsistence
farming

AD 98–117
Roman empire
reaches its
greatest extent

c.500 BC–AD 200
The Nok culture
flourishes.

c.200 Great
Zimbabwe first
settled by Iron
Age people

c.AD 1400

1300–1600
Renaissance in
western Europe.

c.1440–73
Reign of Oba
Ewuare, the Benin
empire-builder.

1526 Foundation
of Mughal empire
in India

1492 Columbus
arrives in America.
Europe begins
period of global
exploration and
colonization.

1807 Britain
outlaws the
slave trade.
European
countries set
up colonies
throughout Africa.

1792–1815
Napoleonic Wars
in Europe

1750–1850
Industrial
Revolution in
the West

1648 Formation
of the Dutch
Republic

1620 Europeans
import the first
slaves into the
Americas

1804 Fulani
Muslim scholar
Usman dan Fodio
starts a popular
revolt in the
Hausa town of
Gudu, which
leads to other
uprisings

1789 Olaudah
Equiano, a freed
slave, publishes
his memoirs

1680–1730 About
20,000 slaves are
exported from
Oyo every year

c.1550

c.1504–50
Reign of Oba
Esigie, who
created the office
of queen mother

1485 The
Portuguese land
on the west
African coast and
encounter the
Benin people

1834 Britain oulaws slavery in all its territories

1837 Queen Victoria comes to the British throne

1861–65 American Civil War

1882 Britain occupies Egypt

1861 Lagos Island is annexed as a colony of Britain

1885 The British declare the Oil Rivers Protectorate, later the Niger Coast Protectorate, in the Niger Delta

1897 The British attack and loot Benin City

2001 The World Trade Center and the Pentagon in the USA are attacked by planes flown by al-Qaeda terrorists

2000 The West celebrates the Millennium – 2000 years since the birth of Christ

1989 Communism collapses in eastern Europe

1986 European countries and the USA impose economic sanctions on South Africa

1980 Britain recognizes the independence of Rhodesia, its last African colony

2003 President Obasanjo is re-elected

1999 Olusegun Obasanjo is elected president

1998 General Abacha dies

1996 Nnamdi Azikiwe, Nigeria's first president, dies

1995 Writer Ken Saro-Wiwa and eight Ogoni activists are hanged

1991 The capital moves from Lagos to Abuja

1979–83 Democracy replaces military rule during the Second Republic

*c.*1900

1914–18 World War One

1929 The Great Depression

1931 Britain establishes the Commonwealth of Nations

1939–45 World War Two

1947 India gains its independence

1906 The British declare the Protectorate of Southern Nigeria

1914 Northern and Southern Nigeria are joined to form the Colony and Protectorate of Nigeria

1929 The 1929 Women's War, a popular uprising against the British

*c.*1980

1967–70 The Biafran War

1966 Widespread rioting; the army takes control

1963 Nigeria is proclaimed a federal republic

*c.*1960

1963–75 The Vietnam War

1960 Nigeria gains its independence

1969 First man lands on the Moon

Glossary

adire Yoruba patterned fabric, dyed indigo

Afro-beat style of music and call-and-response vocal style developed by Nigerian musician Fela Anikulapo-Kuti

archaeologist person who studies the past by excavating ancient cities, sites and artefacts

aso oke fine traditional Yoruba fabric, often kept as a family heirloom

bongo large African antelope with a red-brown coat and white stripes

bushbuck small African antelope

calabash hollow shell of a gourd, used as a rattle

caliph/caliphate Muslim political and religious ruler; land ruled by a caliph

cash crops crops such as coffee grown for export to generate foreign currency, not for domestic consumption

civet greyish, spotted wild African cat, member of same family as genet

civil war war between different sections, political or geographical, of the same nation

colonialism control of one country or people by another

coup sudden overthrow of the government by a small group, often military

deforestation process of clearing land of forest or trees

democracy country or process in which the people choose their government by election, and in which they hold supreme power

desertification change of arable land into desert, either from natural causes or human activity

dialect regional variation of a national language

duikers several types of small African antelope

dynasty succession of rulers belonging to the same family

emir/emirate Muslim ruler; land ruled by an emir

ethnic group racial or linguistic group

fuji style of music based on Yoruba drumming and percussion, popular in Nigeria since the 1970s

genet small, spotted wild African cat, member of same family as civet

gerbil African (and Asian) burrowing rodent with long hind legs and hairy tail

gross national product (GNP) total value of goods and services produced by the people of a country during a period, usually a year

guerilla tactics strategy of using small, independently acting groups in warfare

hartebeest large African antelope with long horns curved backwards at the tips

highlife type of dance music dating from the early 1920s, originally from Ghana and Sierra Leone, that fuses traditional music with European brass band or guitar band music

indigo plant that produces a blue dye; also the colour

Islam religion founded in Arabia in the 7th century and based on the teachings of Muhammad

Islamic relating to or following Islam

juju version of palm-wine music, possibly originally from Lagos, that became popular in the 1940s

klipspringer small, agile yellow-brown antelope

manatee sea cow, type of vegetarian sea mammal with a cigar-shaped body and flipper-like fore limbs

mandrill large, fierce baboon; male has red and blue patches on its face and rump

mangrove tropical tree that grows in swamps or shallow water

minaret tower on mosque from which Muslims are called to prayer

monsoon winds bringing intense rainfall that occurs at the same time every year

Muslim follower of the teachings of Islam

palm-wine music solo guitar music and singing that originated in the palm-wine bars; singers usually sing about current issues

pangolin scaly anteater

papyrus tall, reed-like water plant

poaching hunting or catching wild animals illegally, especially those in protected areas such as national parks and reserves

potto bush baby, slow-moving, large-eyed primate

privatize sell off government-owned industries or concerns to the private sector

republic government in which the citizens of a country hold supreme power and all citizens are equal under the law

savannah large area of arid grassland with sparse trees and bushes

shadoof long pole on a pivot with a bucket at one end and weighted at the other, used to raise water to irrigate land

sitatunga large, dark brown African antelope, also called marshbuck or water kodoe, that lives in swampland and marshy areas; male has spiral horns

sub-Sahara area south of the Sahara Desert

sultan/sultanate Muslim ruler; land ruled by a sultan

treason violation or betrayal of a citizen's allegiance to his or her country or sovereign (ruler)

tributary river or stream that flows into a larger one

warthog grey-brown African wild pig with a large head, long, curved tusks and short legs

Bibliography

Major sources used for this book

Fitzpatrick, Mary, *West Africa* (Lonely Planet Publications, 2002)

Hudgens, Jim and Trillo, Richard, *The Rough Guide to West Africa* (Rough Guides, 1999, 3rd edn)

The Economist, *Pocket World in Figures* (Profile Books, 2003)

General further reading

Bennett, Lynda A. (ed.), *Encyclopedia of World Cultures* (G. K. Hall & Co., 1992)

Student Atlas (Dorling Kindersley, 1998)

The Kingfisher History Encyclopedia. (Kingfisher, 1999)

The World Book Encyclopedia (Scott Fetzer Company, 1999)

World Reference Atlas (Dorling Kindersley, 2000)

Further reading about Nigeria

Achebe, Chinua, *Things Fall Apart* (Penguin Modern Classics, 2001)

Falola, Toyin, *Culture and Customs of Nigeria* (Greenwood Press, 2000)

Maier, Karl, *This House Has Fallen: Midnight in Nigeria* (PublicAffairs, 2000)

Okonta, Ike and Douglas, Oronto, *Where Vultures Feast: Shell, Human Rights, and Oil in the Niger Delta* (Random House, 2001)

Soyinka, Wole, *The Open Sore of a Continent: A Personal Narrative of the Nigerian Crisis* (Oxford University Press, 1997)

Websites about Nigeria

CIA World Factbook
www.cia.gov/cia/publications/factbook/geos/ni.html

News and information about Nigeria, with links to other sites
www.nigeriaworld.com

News, information and current affairs from Nigeria
www.africast.com

Index

Acknowledgements

Cover photo credit
Corbis: Liba Taylor

Photo credits
AKG: 44, 53, Archives CDA/Guillemot 48, Erich Lessing 59t&b; **Brown Reference Group:** 8; **Corbis:** Paul Almasy 18, 97, Bettmann 74, Hulton-Deutsch Collection 73, James Marshall 91; **Empics:** Aubrey Washington 115; **Hutchison Picture Library:** 38, 40, 81, 94, Sarah Errington 78, Maurice G. G. Harvey 83, Juliet Highet 12, 90, 98, 102, A. Howland 27, Liba Taylor 39, 109, Anna Tully 85, Val & Alan Wilkinson 101, J. Reditt 6; **ICCE:** Joe Blossom 99; **Mary Evans Picture Library:** 66; **NASA:** Johnson Space Center 20; **PA Photos:** EPA 116; **photo12.com:** ARJ Collection 58; **Photodisc, Inc:** Stocktrek 30; **Rex Features:** Richard Mildenhall 106, SIPA 77; **Still Pictures:** Adrian Arbib 88, Carlos Guarita 25, 111, Genevieve Renson 29, 34; **Sylvia Cordaiy Photo Library:** Gable 17; **Universal Records:** 105; **Werner Forman Archive Ltd:** British Museum, London 57, 61, 69, Museum fur Volkerkunde, Berlin 62.

How Harmful Are Fossil Fuels?

Catherine Chambers

raintree

a Capstone company — publishers for children

Raintree is an imprint of Capstone Global Library Limited, a company incorporated in England and Wales having its registered office at 7 Pilgrim Street, London, EC4V 6LB – Registered company number: 6695582

www.raintree.co.uk
myorders@raintree.co.uk

Text © Capstone Global Library Limited 2015
The moral rights of the proprietor have been asserted

Edited by Helen Cox Cannons and Jill Kalz
Designed by Steve Mead
Original illustrations © Capstone Global Library Limited 2015
Illustrated by HL Studios, Witney, Oxon
Picture research by Tracy Cummins
Production by Helen McCreath
Originated by Capstone Global Library Limited
Printed and bound in China by CTPS

ISBN 978 1 406 29074 5
18 17 16 15 14
10 9 8 7 6 5 4 3 2 1

British Library Cataloguing in Publication Data
A full catalogue record for this book is available from the British Library.

Acknowledgements
We would like to thank the following for permission to reproduce photographs: We would like to thank the following for permission to reproduce photographs: AP Images: Press Association, 14; Capstone: HL Studios, 5, 6, 20; Corbis: © Adam Burton/Robert Harding World Imagery, 9, © AP Photo/ Charles Rex Arbogast, 31, © Imaginechina, 19, © Tom Fox/Dallas Morning News, 11; Getty Images: ANDEL NGAN/AFP, 10, Arnaldur Halldorsson/Bloomberg, 40, Asim Hafeez/ Bloomberg, 30, 36, Bartek Sadowski/Bloomberg, 21, Central Press/Hulton Archive, 24, Ed Reschke, 4, Norm Betts/Bloomberg, 15, 17, peisen zhao, 22, Ulrich Baumgarten, 39, Wade Payne/Bloomberg, 27, William Thomas Cain, 23; Newscom: Dominique Leppin, 38, T Parisienne/Splash News, 13; Shutterstock: Art Konovalov, 33, bikeriderlondon, 29, fkdkondmi, Cover, Gary Whitton, 35, 37, John Carnemolla, 32, leonello calvetti, Cover, LEXXIZM, 25, Nightman1965, 12, Paul J Martin, 26, puchan, 28, Smileus, 7, straga, 8, Volodymyr Goinyk, 34; Thinkstock: Joe Gough, 16; U.S. Air Force: Joe Davila, 41.

We would like to thank Professor Daniel Block for his invaluable help in the preparation of this book.

Contents

Some words are shown in bold, **like this**. You can find out what they mean by looking in the glossary.

What are fossil fuels?

The burning of fossil fuels – namely coal, oil and natural gas – provides almost 90 per cent of the world's energy. At the moment, we consume more oil than coal or gas, but with new methods of extraction, natural gas is becoming more popular. Many scientists say that exploring, extracting and burning fossil fuels all harm the planet. But is this the whole story? And where will our energy come from if we stop using fossil fuels?

To understand how our use of fossil fuels affects our planet, we must first look at how they formed and where they are found. So, let's go back about 325 million years, when Earth was a warm, swampy place covered in thick vegetation. Prehistoric creatures roamed the land and swam in the seas. Masses of tiny organisms floated on the surface of the oceans. Earth's landmasses heaved with earthquakes, volcanoes and land shifts.

⌃ Ancient fossils of fern-like plants can be found in coal seams.

Gradually, living creatures and plants died in their billions, and were broken down and buried under deep layers of warm mud, sand and rocks. Pressure and extreme heat from Earth's movements transformed some of the dead plant material into reserves of coal. Later, about 298 million years ago, it is thought that simple sea creatures and other living things changed into oil. Natural gas formed alongside coal and oil. Some of these fossil fuels were deposited close to Earth's surface. Others were laid down much deeper, or beneath the ocean floor.

⋁ **This is where we find coal today.**

Coal

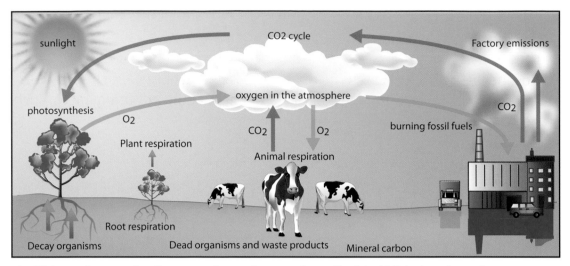

Inside the diagram:

- sunlight
- CO2 cycle
- Factory emissions
- photosynthesis
- oxygen in the atmosphere
- O_2
- CO_2
- Plant respiration
- CO_2
- O_2
- burning fossil fuels
- Animal respiration
- Root respiration
- Decay organisms
- Dead organisms and waste products
- Mineral carbon

⌃ This **carbon cycle** diagram shows how carbon dioxide (CO_2) rises into the atmosphere. Plants back on Earth then absorb the CO_2. Plants use CO_2 and sunlight to make energy for growth.

So how could fossil fuels be a problem?

Most fossil fuels lie deep under layers of rock, sand and mud. Exploring and extracting them can be difficult. The methods and machinery used often harm animals and plants. In turn, this can affect humans who rely on a clean environment for their food or livelihood. Sometimes the visible landscape is scarred, too.

But many countries rely on fossil fuels to keep industry going and increase their wealth. Is this less important than preserving the natural environment and those who depend on it?

> "If you take the Intergovernmental Panel on Climate Change (IPCC) predictions, then by 2040 every summer in Europe will be as hot as it was in 2003 – between 110°F (43°C) and 120°F (49°C). It is not the death of people that is the main problem, it is the fact that the plants can't grow – there will be almost no food grown in Europe."

James Lovelock (born 1919), environmental scientist

What about Earth's atmosphere? All the creatures and plants that were broken down into fossil fuels contained carbons. When coal and oil are burned, these carbons are released as **carbon dioxide** gas that rises into the atmosphere. Some gases are **emitted** when fossil fuels are extracted, such as **methane** gas from coal mining. Burning coal also emits polluting gases, such as **sulphur dioxide**.

Many scientists believe that these gases are a major cause of climate change, especially a rise in global temperature. Later in this book, we shall explore the harmful effects of these gases, and why some scientists do not agree that they cause global warming. But first, how do we extract fossil fuels and what harm might this do?

⌄ These industrial chimneys belch gases that harm the atmosphere or pollute the air we breathe.

What's the harm in extracting coal?

Hard, chunky coal was formed from fern-like plants millions of years ago. It was laid down in thick layers called seams. Some seams are near Earth's surface, while others are buried deep underground. Some lie at different angles, while others lie horizontally. These characteristics lead to different forms of extraction. Coal is a popular fossil-fuel energy source as it is often the cheapest to extract. So, how do we extract coal, and how much harm does this do to the planet?

Some seams lie fairly close to Earth's surface. Machinery removes the layers of rock above these seams to access the coal. This method is called surface, open-pit or opencast mining and is used widely in the UK, Australia, China, South Africa and the United States. The biggest problem is that it destroys the surrounding natural habitat and landscape. The tools and transport used for excavating need fuel, which adds to carbon emissions. Explosives used to access the coal add to the mix of **pollutants**.

⋙ Open-pit coal mining scars the landscape and creates coal dust that can affect people in nearby communities, as well as coal miners.

But surface mining has fewer harmful effects on the health of mineworkers than underground extraction. In many countries, opencast sites use monitoring equipment to check that noise levels and dust from coal and rock do not exceed permitted levels.

It takes 5 to 10 years for an opencast mine like this one to recover and return to nature.

What happens deep underground?

There are different methods of underground mining, depending on the depth of the seam. In deep-shaft mining, modern machinery can now reach coal seams that lie up to 1.5 kilometres (1 mile) beneath the surface. A massive cutter then digs out access tunnels from the shaft. In longwall mining, an automatic, rotating cutter, called a shearing drum, slices up panels of coal that can be as much as 350 metres (383 yards) long.

The harm done by deep mining might not seem as obvious as opencast mining. But the rocks and soil dug out to make shafts and tunnels are deposited at the surface in massive **spoil** heaps. Harmful toxins are brought up with them, polluting the **groundwater** as rainfall washes them into the soil. The ground above deep mines becomes less stable, too.

Did you know?

On 5 August 2010, the main ramp into the San Jose mine in Chile collapsed. Thirty-three miners were trapped over 700 metres (2,300 feet) below ground. No one could contact them for 17 days, and another cave-in blocked the rescue tunnel. The miners survived for 18 days before food and water reached them. They were trapped for 69 days and were finally rescued on 14 October.

⌃ Mountaintop mining companies remove the upper slopes of mountains. The coal waste is often dumped into nearby valleys, harming the natural environment.

∧ In deep mines in South Africa, the air is humid and extremely hot.
Air-conditioning systems help to improve these conditions.

Miners underground are exposed to dust and toxins from the coal and surrounding rock. Gas explosions are another danger. Methane gas rises naturally from the coal as it is mined. Methane is highly explosive and has caused many mine disasters. The worldwide coal-mining industry is trying to reduce the danger by making sure there are plenty of ventilation shafts in mines to allow the methane out, and air to flow in.

Methane gas that reaches the surface can be captured as an energy source. But most is flared, or burned, producing carbon dioxide – a **greenhouse gas**. But as unburned methane is 23 times more likely to increase global warming than carbon dioxide, this should reduce the harm to the atmosphere. It still means that coal extraction is harmful.

Is oil extraction really harmful?

Oil is greasy and viscous, which means it is sticky, runny or oozes. These qualities mean that oil coats everything it comes into contact with. It is also volatile (it catches fire easily) and toxic. These hazards make oil one of the most dangerous fossil fuels to explore and extract. And since the world uses about 90 million barrels of it every day, the planet is exposed to a huge risk of harm. But are the benefits worth the risks? Oil production is still very profitable, and in many places oil costs less to produce than **biofuels** that are grown from plants (see pages 36–37).

Oil reserves often lie deep underneath remote landscapes with rich natural habitats. From sandy deserts and river creeks, to icy oceans and warm seas, oil exploration and extraction can have a huge and lasting impact on people and their environments.

⌄ This oil rig has been towed into Gdansk port in Poland from the open sea. Oil can be spilled while the rig is towed.

⚠ Sea mammals such as this beached whale easily get lost if oil location guns interrupt their senses.

But the problems begin before a single drop of oil is extracted, because even oil exploration can cause harm. To find oil in our oceans, large ships tow huge guns that fire blasts of air into the water, creating sound waves. The sound waves hit the seafloor and bounce back to the ship. Equipment on board analyses the length of the waves. The waves' lengths are mapped out over a large area, giving a picture of the seafloor's rock formations. From this, geologists can see if a particular section of the seafloor is likely to hold oil reserves.

However, this procedure can be highly damaging to marine life – and especially marine mammals such as whales, seals and dolphins. The sound waves disrupt their sense of hearing, which they need to communicate, find their prey and avoid predators.

Did you know?

A single oil survey in the ocean lasts up to three weeks and can cover as much as 966 kilometres (600 miles). The guns used to locate oil can create a sound-wave level of up to 250 decibels. A human ear can be damaged at an 85-decibel level over just eight hours!

Oil exploration on land begins with ground, air and satellite surveys to map the geology of a target area. Computer models show the potential size of the oil fields. Experimental **boreholes** are also drilled, using heavy machinery that churns up the environment and pollutes it with waste spoil from the shaft. However, even greater harm is caused once the drilling begins for real.

What harm can drilling do?

Drilling at sea can cause oil spills and leakages that **contaminate** the ocean and its wildlife, including billions of microscopic plankton that provide food for many sea creatures. Drilling on land can lead to groundwater contamination, as well as wastage when water is used to dislodge blockages in the oil well. All around the sites, the environment is scarred with access roads, lorry tracks, airstrips and buildings.

Did you know?

In the 1980s, the Piper Alpha oil platform off Scotland's North-Sea coast produced over 300,000 barrels of crude oil per day. However, in 1988 a gas leak caused an explosion and a raging fire. It was the worst oil-platform disaster ever recorded. Only 61 out of the 226 workers survived, and it took nearly three weeks to control the flames.

∧∧ Oil riggers often have to work two to three weeks before returning to
shore, and often work at night. They are tested for physical and mental
fitness before they are allowed onto the rig.

What about the harm to workers in the oil industry? Offshore oil platforms,
or rigs, can be dangerous places – especially in areas such as the North Sea,
where there are often severe winter storms. Oil platforms can come adrift or
catch fire. Some helicopters transporting workers to and from the shore have
crashed with tragic loss of life.

BIOGRAPHY

Paul Carter (born 1969)
Paul Carter loved every minute of working on oil platforms
around the world – in the heat of Nigeria's creeks, in Borneo's
tropical rainforest and in the frozen Russian tundra. He loved
the danger and became a popular writer about his experiences.
But Paul is also a keen supporter of cleaner fuels. In 2009,
he rode all around Australia on a motorbike, developed by the
University of Adelaide, that was fuelled by cooking oil.

BIOGRAPHY

**Kenule "Ken" Beeson Saro Wiwa
(1941–1995)**

The writer Ken Saro Wiwa protested against damage caused by oil exploration in his Ogoni homeland in Nigeria. In the Niger Delta, oil spills have polluted mangrove swamps, fishing habitats and farmland. The United Nations suggests it will take US$1 billion and 30 years to clean up the Niger Delta. Saro Wiwa used poetry and peaceful protest to get the world's attention.

∨ This is an oil refinery in Australia. Oil has to be refined, or cleaned up, before it can be used. Oil refineries can produce a lot of toxic wastewater sludge.

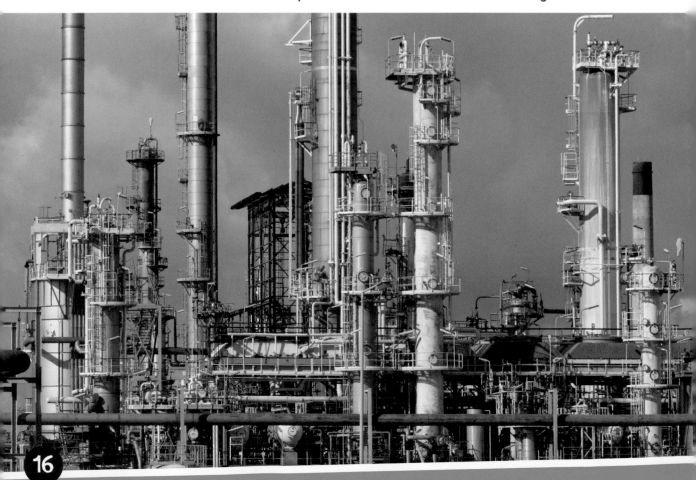

How harmful is oil transportation?

We sometimes see the disastrous results of major oil leaks, spills and fires on the television news. Most of these accidents happen while oil is being transported from wells to refineries and then to power plants or service stations in tankers, pipelines and lorries.

One of the biggest spills occurred in 1989 when the tanker *Exxon Valdez* split open, spilling 41.8 million litres (11 million gallons) of oil, and damaging 2,092 kilometres (1,300 miles) of Alaskan coastline. However, some experts in oil exploration believe that oil theft from pipelines causes as much harm to the environment as oil spills. Nevertheless, between 1970 and 2013, 5.74 million tonnes of oil were spilled from tankers alone. Some of the biggest spills have happened during wars, such as the First Gulf War in Kuwait. The rest is natural seepage from oil sources.

Did you know?

Plans are in place to build the 1,897-kilometre (1,179-mile) Keystone XL oil pipeline from Canada's tar sands to the United States. The tar sands shown here are in Alberta, Canada. There's a danger that many oil leaks could occur in such a long pipeline. Oil from tar sands is extracted from thick, sticky bitumen mixed with sand. The extraction process pollutes nearby habitats and emits a lot of carbon dioxide. But extracting oil and tar from sand is increasingly popular as other oil reserves become harder to reach.

What's the harm in extracting gas?

Can exploring, extracting and transporting natural gas harm the planet? Many environmentalists would argue that it can. Yet the gas industry and some governments argue that gas is a "clean energy" because gas does not release much carbon dioxide when it is burned. Who is right? Natural gas is as cheap to extract as oil, so can we afford to stop exploiting it?

As with oil exploration, the size of a natural gas field is assessed using ground, air and satellite imaging, and computer modelling. There is also experimental drilling. Computer models are not always right, so drilling stops if the gas field turns out to be small. On land, this leaves a lot of holes, toxic spoil heaps and a damaged habitat.

Did you know?

Researchers from Boston University and North Carolina's Duke University in the United States have located almost 6,000 gas leaks in Washington DC's underground pipeline system. Risks are high and include explosions and health hazards.

Established gas fields cause similar hazards to the environment – only on a much larger scale. Soil erosion is added to the mix. As gas is explored, toxins are drawn up with water, mud and sludge and are contained in nearby evaporation ponds and pits. During the drilling itself, one of the most hazardous toxins is **radioactive** radon gas, which occurs naturally in rocks and soils around the gas pocket. Site workers inhaling the gas are at increased risk of lung cancer.

⌃ A new pipeline stretches over 700 kilometres (435 miles) from Myanmar to China.
Environmentalists fear for sensitive marine, mountain and forest habitats.

Surely gas cannot pollute as much as oil?

Gas pollution is silent and invisible – but it is real! Gas is especially dangerous
during transportation and processing. During processing, impurities from
the natural gas are removed. These impurities include **hydrogen sulphide**,
helium, carbon dioxide, other non-methane **hydrocarbons** and moisture, and
they are harmful if they escape. Pipelines then transport the gas to power
plants. Any fractures in the pipes can leak out dangerous methane emissions.

What's the fuss about fracking?

Many people from all parts of the world are protesting against fracking. So, what are their concerns? Fracking is hydraulic fracturing. In this process, water pressure is used to break up rock, releasing minute pockets of natural gas. The type of rock holding the gas is called Marcellus shale, a layer that lies at least 1.6 kilometres (1 mile) underground.

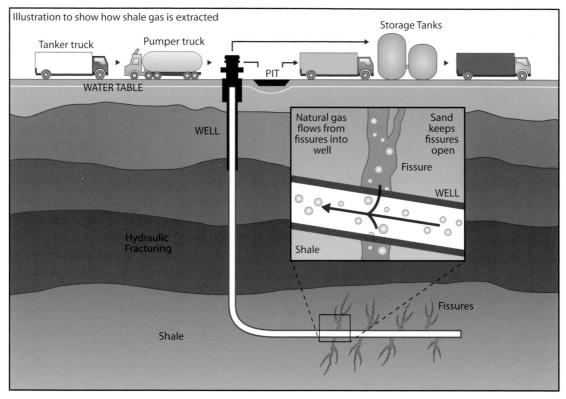

Illustration to show how shale gas is extracted

⌃ Most of the fracking process is underground and unseen. This means it is hard to assess the environmental impact.

Did you know?

In Texas, USA, media reports claimed that during November 2013, 16 earthquakes rocked the state. Many blamed fracking. But geologists at the United States Geological Survey believe that dumping the wastewater from fracking deep underground in empty wells could be the problem.

Each well is drilled vertically until the shale is reached. Then it is drilled horizontally along the band of shale for a distance of about 400 metres (a quarter of a mile). This broad band of rock is then shattered by up to 23 million litres (6 million gallons) of water plus sand and chemicals to expose the gas.

Those who oppose fracking argue that it can cause air and groundwater pollution, including radioactivity from wastewater. Fracking has also been blamed for earth tremors. Exploring and exploiting shale gas requires a lot of heavy machinery that disturbs nearby residents and wildlife. Shale workers on site are exposed to toxins, such as silica dust, that can cause lung diseases.

⌄ **This fracking site is in the province of Lublin in Poland.**

How harmful is burning coal today?

Coal burns with a bright, hot flame that has brought warmth and light to people for hundreds of years. It fuelled steam engines and the birth of the railway. **Coke**, a form of burned coal, was used to smelt iron to build ships and machinery. But as the numbers of factories and trains increased, so did the volume of emissions. Coal's toxic soot emissions stuck to buildings – and inside human lungs. The development of coal-fired power stations added to the problem.

Coal creates the most harmful emissions of all the fuels used in power stations. Each coal-fired power station produces nearly twice as much carbon dioxide as it does natural gas, plus 12 times the amount of sulphur dioxide and five times the amount of **nitrogen oxide** for the amount of energy created. Some types of coal, called "high sulphur", have been cleaned so that they are less harmful. But they still emit damaging gases. What do these gases do?

⌄ This modern iron-smelting furnace injects a less harmful type of **pulverised coal**. Coal pollutes less than coke in the iron-smelting process.

⋀ This 19th-century stone house in Bath, England, has not yet been cleaned up after years of past coal burning, which polluted the air.

We know about the link between increased carbon-dioxide levels and climate change. However, sulphur dioxide affects us at ground level, increasing breathing problems such as asthma.

When nitrogen oxide combines with other **compounds**, it reacts with sunlight to create ground-level **ozone gas**. This causes severe breathing problems for some people. Nitrogen oxide harms the atmosphere, too. It is one of the gases that destroy the atmosphere's **ozone layer**, which protects Earth from the Sun's harmful rays. Levels of these gases have shrunk over the last 40 years in places where power plants have captured and recycled the gases.

Did you know?

How do power plants work? Firstly, they need fuel to burn, such as coal. The heat from the burning coal boils water to create steam. The steam rises and presses against the blades of turbines, making them spin. The blades are connected to generators that create electricity.

Sulphur dioxide and nitrogen oxide become even more harmful when they react with water, oxygen and other chemicals in the atmosphere and fall as "acid rain" – or acid hail or snow. When this toxic substance mixes with fog it forms a thick, polluting, deadly smog.

London's Great Smog of 1952, in which an estimated 4,000 people died, led to the UK's Clean Air Acts of 1956, 1968 and 1993. UK law now insists that only low-smoke coals, such as anthracite, are burned in crowded city areas.

Eyewitness

During the Great London Smog, which began on 4 December 1952, there was no escaping the foul-smelling, sulphurous air. Stan Cribb, an undertaker, remembers, "You couldn't see a hand in front of you. Not only did you have this thick, black, curling smoke – it crept in everywhere, even the home – lace curtains thick with this oily substance."

But in many countries there are no such laws, or they are poorly enforced. For example, coal emissions contribute to China's estimated 350,000 deaths each year from air pollution.

⌄ Acid rain can fall on lakes and coastal bays, reducing oxygen in the water. Fish and marine plants need oxygen to survive. Water quickly becomes stagnant without it.

What happens to heaps of ash waste?

Coal-fired power-plant sites contain heaps of ash waste that can fill nearby ponds with toxic **metal oxides** and **alkalis**. In addition, the great mounds of coal on these sites contain traces of arsenic and lead. Falling rain soaks through the coal heaps, and may trickle into river systems and lakes, carrying harmful toxins to fish and other wildlife. The toxins may also soak into the soil and pollute the groundwater. But even worse things can happen.

⌃ China plans to build 160 new coal-fired power plants, adding to the 620 already operating. The country is searching for new technology to help reduce emissions.

Did you know?

In 2012, the International Energy Agency published a list of the world's top ten coal producers. China heads the list.

Top ten world coal producers, in millions of tonnes			
PR China	3,471	Russia	334
USA	1,004	South Africa	253
India	585	Germany	189
Australia	414	Poland	139
Indonesia	376	Kazakhstan	117

⌃ Ash sludge from the Tennessee Valley Authority (TVA) Kingston coal-plant spill polluted the land with toxic metals.

On 22 December 2008, an enormous ash spill occurred at the TVA Kingston coal-fired power plant in Harriman, Tennessee, USA. After 10 days of ceaseless rain, a wall holding back a spoil heap of toxic ash sludge collapsed. It flooded 12 homes, flowed into a nearby lake and polluted the Emory River, killing hundreds of fish. It is estimated that over 3.8 billion litres (1 billion gallons) of ash sludge spilled over 121 hectares (300 acres).

HERO OR VILLAIN?

Coal and coal products have created a lot of wealth. Some of the emissions they produce are now recycled. For example, ash is used in cement and other building materials. Coking coal, vital in steel production, has excellent heat-shielding properties, too. New energy-saving coke-fuelled steel furnaces have also been developed.

Does burning oil harm the planet?

Where would we be without oil? It gives us light and heat, as well as energy for industry. It fuels vehicles that allow us to travel quickly and in comfort. But what harm is our use of oil doing to the planet – and to us?

Does driving motor vehicles cause more harm than any other use of oil? Most scientists say it does. Firstly, burning petrol and **diesel oil** creates gas emissions from vehicles' exhaust systems. These gases include carbon dioxide, carbon monoxide, sulphur dioxide, nitrogen oxide and water vapour. Secondly, vehicles emit particulates, which are minute pieces of solid matter.

⌄ Jet aircraft today emit fewer harmful gases per journey than they did 50 years ago. But there are a lot more journeys!

Did you know?

Crude oil is processed into several different fuels: petrol and diesel fuel for road vehicles, jet fuel for aircraft, heating fuel and **liquefied petroleum gas** (**LPG**), which can be used in vehicles or for heating. Each fuel emits different quantities of harmful gases.

We breathe in all these substances – and more! If we are exposed to a lot of them over a long period of time, they can increase our risk of heart disease, asthma and lung cancer. People who are already ill are at more risk. So, too, are the very young and the very old.

Which fuel causes the most harm? Diesel was once thought to be a cleaner fuel than petrol because it emits less carbon dioxide. But it's been discovered that diesel fumes contain harmful pollutants that petrol does not – some of which are more likely to cause cancers. Diesel fumes can also create smog.

<< Oil-fired power plants are expensive to build and maintain.

Do oil-fired power plants harm the planet?

Oil-fired power plants generate large amounts of energy very quickly. They can be built anywhere that has good transport links and a generous supply of water for cooling. But as well as greenhouse gas emissions, oil-fired power stations create toxic sludge and wastewater from cooling. These waste products are hard to clean up, recycle or throw away.

What happens when we burn oil waste?

Fierce debates surround the type of oil extracted from Canada's tar sands (see page 17). This thick, sticky bitumen oil needs to be thinned and graded in special refineries before it can be burned. This produces emissions and wastes that are hard to dispose of.

A particular problem is the hard, coal-like, waste substance called "petcoke" (petroleum coke). When it burns, petcoke emits several times more carbon dioxide and sulphur dioxide than the oil from which it comes. Canada and the United States will not use petcoke, so it is exported to developing countries for them to burn instead. This adds to these countries' carbon footprints and health problems.

HERO OR VILLAIN?

Some climatologists say that **nuclear-fuelled** power plants are cleaner than oil-fired plants and would be less harmful to the planet. But nuclear plants use **uranium**, which is non-renewable and hazardous. Nuclear waste is radioactive, highly dangerous and hard to dispose of safely. Which would you choose?

The USA needs to import nearly 9 billion barrels of oil a day and burns almost 1,000 billion kilograms (1 billion metric tons) of coal every year. So some leaders in industry and government are in no hurry to stop refining and using tar sands oil just because it produces petcoke. Do the needs outweigh the harm?

⌄ Canada has nearly 78 million tonnes (85 million tons) of petcoke piles. One oil refinery in Detroit, USA, processes 28,000 barrels of tar-sands oil per day, creating nearby spoil heaps. In Chicago, petcoke piles have caused alarming levels of toxic dust and runoff into rivers.

Is natural gas a "clean" form of energy?

The natural gas industry claims that it is a very clean form of energy. When burned, it produces less of the greenhouse gas carbon dioxide than other fossil fuels. It has low nitrogen oxide and produces virtually no sulphur dioxide emissions or mercury, so it won't contribute to poor air quality, smog or polluted waterways. But is this the whole story?

Natural gas is made up mostly of methane. This has a Global Warming Potential (GWP) 20 times that of carbon dioxide over a 100-year timescale. But this is only if it escapes as it is being explored, transported, stored, or if there are leaks at gas power plants. Even then, methane is thought to last in the atmosphere for only 20 years, which is many times less than carbon dioxide.

⌄ Methane gases from livestock make up about 10 per cent of Australia's greenhouse gases. Cattle from northern Australia produce half of this amount!

HERO OR VILLAIN?

Natural gas is not the only fuel that leaks methane. Petroleum oil and coal do, too. Together, they produce over 40 per cent of all methane emissions in the United States. But the rest comes from natural sources such as decaying bacteria in wetlands, decaying matter in landfill sites and a lot from stomach gases of livestock such as cattle!

But what harm does natural gas do when it is burned? Natural gas power stations still emit carbon dioxide through their chimneys. The burning process produces a lot of polluted wastewater that gets discharged into rivers and lakes. In the home, gas heating and cooking systems emit toxins that are harmful to the lungs, including tiny solid particles, carbon monoxide and nitrogen oxide.

⋙ There is a lot of pressure to change lorry fuel from diesel to natural gas. But many scientists argue that unless methane leaks are plugged, natural gas will be a worse pollutant than diesel.

What can we use instead of fossil fuels?

What will we do when fossil fuels run out? Will this be a blessing to the planet? Or will it just mean that we are poorer? Some energy companies have developed alternatives. Others, however, are trying new ways of finding fossil fuels in the toughest parts of the planet. Which way will it go? And which will do the least harm?

" **Those who argue that we should stop exploring, harvest existing fields, and block new opportunities are, at best, preparing for a future that doesn't exist...** "

Helge Lund, Chief Executive Officer of the energy company Statoil, speaking in 2013

⌄ In Antarctica, melting ice would make oil and gas exploration much easier. Will it ever happen?

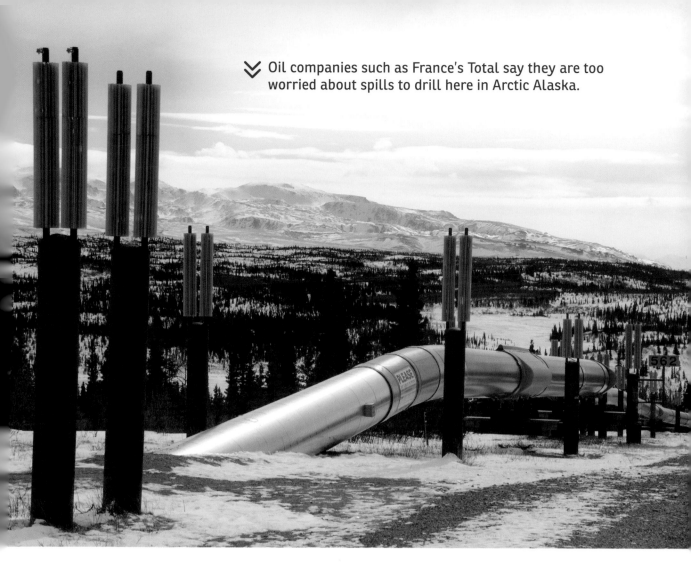

Oil companies such as France's Total say they are too worried about spills to drill here in Arctic Alaska.

When will fossil fuels run out? Many who are in favour of fossil fuels believe that they will last for a very long time because new sources are constantly being found. Those who prefer carbon-free energy say they'll all be gone by 2088! But, for now, fossil fuel exploration is taking place in some of the most sensitive natural environments, including the Arctic. Here, many local communities worry about the **ecological** effects of leaks and spills.

Is the clean, wild Antarctic region safe? So far, the area is protected from mining by an agreement called the Madrid Protocol that was signed in 1998 by all countries with an interest in the region. However, the ban on mining in the Antarctic will be reviewed in 2048. Do you think the need for fuels will win over protecting the environment?

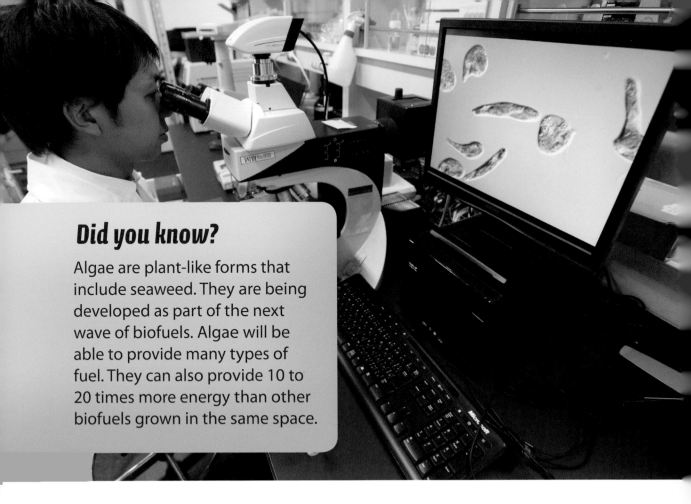

What's the harm in growing fuels?

Are plants the answer? Wood has provided fuel since humans discovered how to make fire. Wood is still a useful fuel as long as trees can be grown like a crop and replaced. However, as a fuel, wood emits a lot of carbon dioxide.

Nowadays, other crops are grown for fuel called biofuels. They can be used to power both industry and vehicles. Some plants, such as sugarcane and wheat, produce sugar and starch that is fermented to make **ethanol**. Other crops, such as soya beans, corn and palms, produce oils that are made into **biodiesel**. Biofuels can also be made from decaying waste plant and animal material. All these fuels together are known as **biomass**.

There are a lot of advantages to growing biofuels. Many scientists believe they are "carbon neutral" and will not contribute to climate change. Biofuels are also renewable.

However, there are also problems. Growing crops for biofuels takes up land that could be used for growing food. Large biofuel agricultural companies have pushed out smaller farmers. Big areas of rainforest have been cleared to make way for biofuel crops. Rainforests can absorb extra carbon dioxide from the atmosphere, and cutting them back could affect the world's climates.

Ploughing, sowing and applying chemical fertilizers, pesticides and herbicides all add to pollution and the carbon footprint of biofuels. They also use up a great deal of water. However, scientists are looking at ways of making fuels from the stalks of harvested crops, so no extra water or land would be needed.

⌄ In Brazil, sugarcane is grown to make ethanol.

What about wind, waves, water and sun?

For hundreds of years people used the power of wind and water to drive the windmills and watermills that ground grain into flour. Today, we generate **hydroelectric power** (**HEP**) from fast-flowing river water as it passes through huge dams. Wind turbines and wave barriers along coastlines add to the power supply. The Sun's energy can be converted to electricity through **photovoltaic cells**. Wind, waves, water and sunshine are all renewable sources of energy. So, what could be the problem?

Let us start with dams. When a dam is built to block the flow of a river, a vast lake of water builds up behind it. Electricity is generated when water from the lake is released through the dam and plunges downwards, turning electric turbines below. But these huge, man-made lakes have flooded river valleys, destroyed wildlife and freshwater habitats, and forced people to leave their homes. Dams can also cut off water supplies further down the river. For example, there are worries that Turkey's plans to dam the Euphrates and Tigris rivers will reduce water supplies to Syria and Iraq, which lie downstream.

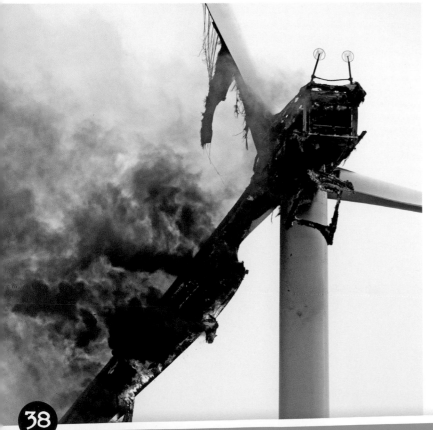

« When really strong winds hit wind turbines, there is a danger they can catch fire.

⌃ Solar energy can power refrigerators and stoves in remote areas. Clinics can store vaccines in refrigerators to keep them fresh.

We can now harness the power of waves by anchoring turbines offshore in rows stretching across coastal bays. But protestors say that the turbines disrupt the habitat of sea creatures, and harm the fishing industry.

Solar panels still cannot harness the Sun's energy at all times. It takes a lot of panels, and therefore a lot of land, to generate a strong, steady supply of electricity. Wind farms are also unable to supply more than a small percentage of our energy needs – and protestors complain that they ruin the landscape.

So how harmful are fossil fuels?

We know that most scientists believe that burning fossil fuels causes or contributes to climate change. We know that when we exploit fossil fuels, humans and habitats are harmed. But we also know that alternative forms of energy cannot yet replace them. Fossil fuels are easier to use than nuclear fuel, and can produce more energy for the same amount of effort as renewable fuels. So what is the way forward?

> **Horses create 772 grams of pollution per kilometre travelled (for each horse galloping), modern cars only 72.4 grams per kilometre. The wellsite footprint for (oil) wells drilled at Prudhoe Bay (Alaska) has been reduced from 60 acres to 6 acres since 1970.**

Lee Gerhard (born 1937), retired geologist and climate change **sceptic**, 2001

⋁ There is a lot of volcanic activity in Iceland, which is used to produce **geothermal energy**.

Could rocket science help find fuels for Earth? A new rocket fuel called ALICE is being developed using aluminium powder and water ice.

We can all try to reduce our use of fossil fuels. We could travel by train, bus or bicycle more often, and so reduce the number of cars on the roads. We could insulate our homes better so that we use less heating – or wear extra warm layers! We could remember to turn off lights and other electrical equipment when they are not in use. And we could reuse and recycle more household items to help cut down on fuels used to produce new goods. These are just a few of the things we could do to help.

But what about poorer countries that are trying to increase their wealth by developing their industries? Industry needs power, and these countries cannot afford to wait for cheap and effective alternatives to fossil fuels. There are no easy answers to the harm or problems created by fossil fuels.

Quiz

How much do you remember about fossil fuels from reading this book? You could find out by answering these questions. You can use the index to help you. Some of the answers might lie in the boxes and captions as well as the main text.

1   Which of these gases is not a fossil fuel?
    A   coal
    B   natural gas
    C   ethanol
    D   petroleum oil

2   What harm do too many greenhouse gases in Earth's atmosphere do?
    A   they poison the air that we breathe
    B   they help plants to grow in greenhouses
    C   they are thought to contribute to climate change
    D   they stop the Sun's rays from reaching Earth

3   Which type of petroleum oil is thick, sticky and mixed with sand before it is processed?
    A   oil found deep under the ocean
    B   biofuel oil
    C   oil that gets mixed with sand as it is transported
    D   Tar sands oil

4   What type of machine is used to extract coal in the underground longwall mining method?
    A   A pickaxe
    B   A pneumatic drill
    C   A rotating shearing drum
    D   A triangular coal plough

5   The long 2,700 kilometre (1,678 mile) Keystone XL oil pipeline is being built between which two countries?
    A   Australia and New Zealand
    B   Canada and the USA
    C   Russia and Canada
    D   The UK and Poland

6 How far underground is Marcellus shale, a type of rock mined when fracking?

A 1.6 kilometres
B 1.4 kilometres
C 2.6 kilometres
D 2.5 kilometres

7 Energy plants powered by nuclear fuel are considered cleaner than those powered by fossil fuels. But which of these problems does nuclear fuel create?

A Nuclear fuel emits methane gas
B Nuclear fuel creates dangerous radioactive waste
C Nuclear fuel emits gases that cause lung disease
D Nuclear fuel creates sooty particulates

8 Particulates are emitted by burning fossil fuels. What are they and what harm do they do?

A They are ozone gases that rise into the Stratosphere, destroying the ozone layer
B They are pieces of coal that can burn plants
C They are greenhouse gases that can cause climate change
D They are tiny solids, mainly carbons, that are released into the air, causing lung disease

9 Which gas causes breathing problems and acid rain when coal is burned?

A Carbon dioxide is the cause
B Sulphur dioxide is the cause
C Oxygen is the cause
D Helium is the cause

10 Coal, oil and natural gas produce 40 per cent of all harmful methane gases released on Earth. What else releases methane gas?

A The stomachs of plant-eating livestock such as cattle
B Rainforest trees
C Photovoltaic cells used to create solar energy
D Wind farms

ANSWERS: 1C, 2C, 3D, 4C, 5B, 6A, 7B, 8D, 9B, 10A

43

Glossary

alkali chemical in burned coal waste that can be toxic in water sources and in soil

biodiesel biofuel that can be used in diesel engines

biofuel renewable fuel made from plant matter

biomass fuels created using plant and animal matter

borehole deep hole drilled by miners

carbon cycle movement of carbon gases in a circle, emitted from carbon gases and absorbed by plant life and carbon sinks such as the oceans

carbon dioxide greenhouse gas released by burning fossil fuels; also one of several impure gases removed from natural gas fuel before it is used

coke type of coal made by burning coals, such as bituminous coal

compound substance made up of two or more chemical elements

contaminate when a toxic substance mixes with water, air or soil, making it stale or poisonous

diesel oil fuel that is usually extracted from petroleum oil and used in diesel engines; it can also be extracted from plants (biodiesel)

ecological the relation of living organisms to each other and their habitats

emit produce and give out something, usually a gas

ethanol biofuel made by fermenting starch from a plant, such as wheat

geothermal energy energy from volcanic sources

greenhouse gas gas that causes climate change, particularly global warming

groundwater underground water source

helium type of impure gas removed from natural gas fuel before it is used

hydrocarbon type of impure gas removed from natural gas fuel before it is used

hydroelectric power (HEP) power source that uses the force of water to turn turbines and create electric power

hydrogen sulphide type of impure gas removed from natural gas fuel before it is used

liquefied petroleum gas (LPG) type of gas from refined petroleum oil or certain forms of natural gas. We usually burn LPG on camping stoves.

metal oxide chemical in burned coal waste that can be toxic in water sources and in soil

methane greenhouse gas released by burning fossil fuels

nitrogen oxide polluting gas found in car exhausts

non-renewable fuel type that can no longer be formed naturally or created artificially

nuclear fuel radioactive energy created by using uranium and plutonium chemical elements

ozone gas gas that can rise into the atmosphere and destroy the ozone layer

ozone layer layer of gases in the stratosphere that protects Earth from the Sun's harmful rays

photovoltaic cell manufactured cell in which the Sun's energy can be stored and used as a power source

pollutant toxic substance that can be harmful to the natural world, humans and the atmosphere

pulverised coal powdered coal or coal dust

radioactive substance used in nuclear fuels that can create harmful rays if it is leaked

renewable fuel type that is formed naturally, for example wind energy

sceptic someone who questions or doubts accepted opinions about a subject

solar panel panel of photovoltaic cells in which energy from the Sun can be stored and used

spoil waste from extracting or burning fossil fuels

sulphur dioxide polluting gas released by burning coal

uranium radioactive chemical element used in creating nuclear fuels

wellsite footprint amount of carbon emissions and damage around a wellsite

Find out more

If you want to find out more about fossil fuels, why not take a look at some of these books, websites and places to visit.

Books

Energy Resources (Maps of the Environmental World series), Jack Gillett and Meg Gillett (Wayland, 2011)

Fossil Fuel Power (Let's Discuss Energy Resources), Richard and Louise Spilsbury (Wayland, 2010)

Fossil Fuels (A World After), Liz Gogerly (Raintree, 2013)

Fossil Fuels (Sci-Hi), Eve Hartman and Wendy Meshbesher (Raintree, 2010)

Websites

www.carbonkids.net/kids_fossilfuels.html
Visit this website for facts, figures, fun, and quizzes that will help you learn more about fossil fuels.

www.childrensuniversity.manchester.ac.uk/interactives/science/energy/renewable
Find out about renewable and non-renewable energy on the Children's University of Manchester website.

www.clean-air-kids.org.uk/globalwarming.html
Learn all about global warming on this website.

www.kids.esdb.bg/geothermal.html
Find out more about climate change on this web page.

Places to visit

Local and national science and technology museums often hold special exhibitions on the atmosphere, the environment and climate change. You can also check out the following:

Science Museum, London
www.sciencemuseum.org.uk
Among the many great science exhibits in this museum there is a display called "Climate Changing Stories". It looks at climate over time through scientific discovery, artefacts and art.

Natural History Museum, London
www.nhm.ac.uk/index.html
Explore the Earth Today and Tomorrow gallery, which looks at Earth's natural resources and shows how we can live in a more sustainable way, without spoiling our planet. There are displays of wind, wave and solar powered technology, which could help reduce the wild weather associated with burning fossil fuels and climate change. See how strong winds, waves and weather affect our planet in the Restless Surface gallery.

Dynamic Earth, Edinburgh
www.dynamicearth.co.uk/learning
Here, you can find out more about the science of our planet, including climate change, through 3D and 4D technology and interactive exhibitions. Workshops, outdoor activities and a fun zone bring learning to life. You can see how earth developed over time and how it might evolve in the future. From Space, you can look down at Earth and see in what ways humans have changed the planet.

Thinktank Birmingham Science Museum
www.thinktank.ac
Find out more about Earth and the environment in this museum's Science Garden and Digital Planetarium.

Index

Howling Hurricanes

Heinemann
LIBRARY

Louise and Richard Spilsbury

www.heinemann.co.uk/library
Visit our website to find out more information about **Heinemann Library** books.

To order:
 Phone 44 (0) 1865 888066
Send a fax to 44 (0) 1865 314091
 Visit the Heinemann Bookshop at www.heinemann.co.uk/library to browse our catalogue and order online.

First published in Great Britain by
Heinemann Library, Halley Court,
Jordan Hill, Oxford OX2 8EJ, part of
Harcourt Education.
Heinemann is a registered trademark of
Harcourt Education Ltd.

Editorial: Andrew Farrow and Dan Nunn
Design: David Poole and Paul Myerscough
Illustrations: Geoff Ward
Picture Research: Rebecca Sodergren and
Debra Weatherley
Production: Viv Hichens

Originated by Dot Gradations Limited
Printed in Hong Kong, China by
Wing King Tong

ISBN 0 431 17835 6
08 07 06 05 04
10 9 8 7 6 5 4 3 2 1

**British Library Cataloguing in
Publication Data**
Spilsbury, Richard, 1963 –
Howling hurricanes. – (Awesome forces
of nature)
1. Hurricanes – Juvenile literature
I. Title II. Spilsbury, Louise
551.5'52
A full catalogue record for this book is
available from the British Library.

Acknowledgements
The publishers would like to thank the
following for permission to reproduce
photographs:

Associated Press pp. **13** (Jose Goitia), **20**
(John McConnico), **23** (Victor Caivano), **26**
(Bob Coates), **28**; Corbis/Bettmann pp. **10**,
24; Getty News and Sport p. **14**; NASA
p. **25**; NOAA pp. **5** (Fema), **19**, **21**; Panos
p. **6** (Bruce Paton); Reuters pp. **9**, **15**, **27**;
Rex Features pp. **16** (Peter Heismath), **17**
(Sipa); Science Photo Library pp. **7**, **18**
(NASA/Goddard Space Flight Centre); Still
Pictures p. **22** (Julio Etchart); Trip pp. **4**
(Viesti Collection), **8** (NASA).

Cover photograph reproduced courtesy of
Reuters/Jorge Silva.

Every effort has been made to contact
copyright holders of any material
reproduced in this book. Any omissions will
be rectified in subsequent printings if notice
is given to the publishers.

Contents

*Any words appearing in the text in bold, **like this**, are explained in the Glossary.*

What is a hurricane?

Hurricanes are the most powerful storms on Earth. They grow from **tropical** storms over the sea. Some stay over the open ocean, far from land, and some weaken and die out before they reach land. Others hurtle towards a shore at high speed.

Hurricane winds often travel at speeds of up to 350 kilometres per hour – faster than the quickest train on Earth! If hurricanes reach land, their violent, fast winds and heavy rain can cause terrible damage and destruction. Some only last for days, others can go on for weeks. Hurricanes usually cause most damage around coasts, but big hurricanes can sometimes reach far inland.

These waves are being whipped up by a Caribbean hurricane. The word 'hurricane' is said to come from the name of a god of evil, 'Hurican'. People in the Caribbean in the past gave it this name because of its destructive power.

Hurricanes cause great destruction when they move onto land. They can blow down buildings, pull up trees and throw cars and boats around like toys. They also whip up the sea to form giant waves that crash onto shores. Heavy rains can cause floods, when land that is normally dry is covered in water. In the past, hurricanes killed many people. Today **scientists** usually spot dangerous hurricanes early and warn people to move to a safe place.

Naming hurricanes

Scientists give hurricanes boys' and girls' names. They do this so that everyone who talks about a particular hurricane, whether they are scientists or ordinary people, know which one it is. The names go in alphabetical order, but scientists don't use Q, U, X, Y or Z as there are few names starting with these letters.

This is just some of the damage caused by Hurricane Camille, which hit the USA in August 1969.

How do hurricanes happen?

Hurricanes always begin over warm water. Warm water heats up the air just above it. When air heats up, it becomes lighter and it rises up higher in the sky. When the layer of warm air moves up, cooler air fills the space it has left. This causes winds.

Over **tropical** waters that reach very high temperatures, the heat makes the air rise very quickly. As the winds and clouds rise, they move faster and faster. They also start to **rotate** in a spiral. When the winds in this spinning storm reach about 120 kilometres per hour, it is called a hurricane. The whirling pattern of the winds makes the air inside the hurricane move even faster.

Hurricanes may begin like this – as winds that merely whip up waves on the sea. A hurricane usually takes days to develop. The fastest a hurricane might form is two days.

How do hurricanes die?

Hurricanes are created and powered by the heat that comes off very warm water. As hurricanes move over land which is cooler than the sea, or over cooler stretches of water, they weaken and start to die out. A hurricane without warm water is like a toy car with a run-down battery – it gradually loses power and then stops altogether.

Top hurricane speeds

No one really knows exactly how fast the fastest hurricanes go because measuring equipment is often destroyed by the hurricane. Some **scientists** believe that the fastest hurricane winds are around 300 kilometres an hour, while others say they might reach almost 600 kilometres per hour!

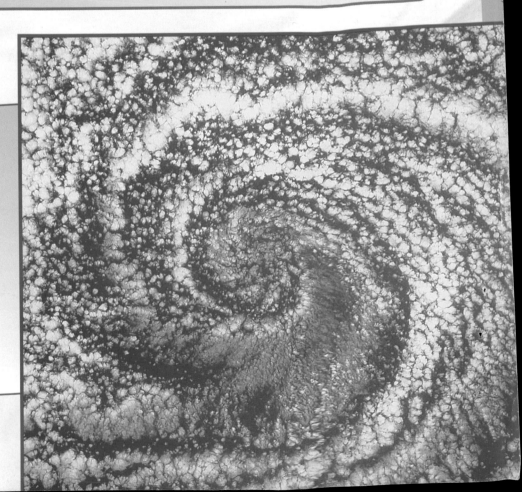

If fast enough, winds above a warm sea can start spinning within 12 hours. You can see the winds spiralling fast in this picture from above a hurricane, taken from the Space Shuttle.

What is a hurricane's eye?

The **eye** of a hurricane is at its centre, inside the swirling mass of wind and cloud. If you could fly high above a hurricane and look down inside it, it would look like water spinning out of a plughole. The centre is calm and the strongest winds spin around it in the **eyewall**. When the eye passes over land, people below feel just a gentle breeze and the rain stops. As the hurricane moves on, the winds at the edge of the eye – the eyewall – begin again.

Making a mini-hurricane eye

You can create your own mini-hurricane eye after a bath. When the water spirals around the plug hole, right in the middle there is a dry centre. This is just like the eye of a hurricane, except that in a hurricane you get huge spiralling winds and clouds instead of swirling water.

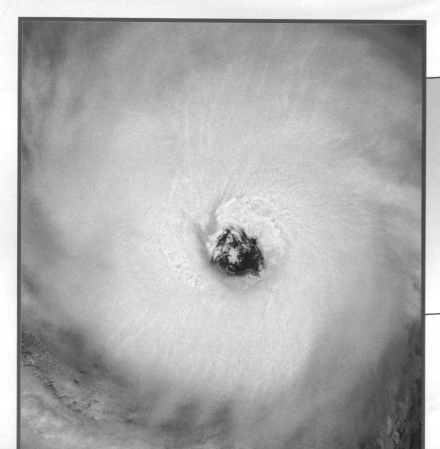

This photo was taken directly over the eye of a hurricane. Most hurricanes have an eye between 30–60 kilometres (18–37 miles) across.

How do hurricane rains form?

Hurricanes almost always bring very heavy rains. Hurricanes do this because as they travel across oceans they suck water up into the sky. They do this by a process called **evaporation**. Evaporation happens when water warms up to a certain temperature. Then it stops being a liquid and it turns into a gas in the air, called water vapour. This is how wet clothes dry outside after washing. The water inside them is warmed by the air and evaporates, leaving the clothes dry.

Water vapour turns back into water when it cools down. Hurricane winds cool down when they get nearer land and further away from the warm oceans. This is when the vapour they are carrying turns back into liquid. It falls from the sky as heavy rain.

Large hurricanes can carry vast amounts of water vapour. This means that they can cause incredibly heavy rainstorms, like this one during Hurricane Keith, which hit Belize in October 2000.

Where do hurricanes happen?

Hurricanes only start over really warm water, so they only form in certain parts of the world. Hurricanes never start over cold oceans, such as the South Atlantic. They form over **tropical** oceans. These areas of water are near the **Equator**, an imaginary line around the centre of the Earth, where it is always very warm.

When is a hurricane not a hurricane?

Hurricanes are called different names in different parts of the world. These storms are called hurricanes when they happen over the North Atlantic and Northeast Pacific oceans. When they occur in the Pacific and Indian Oceans they are called typhoons or cyclones. Even though they have different names, they are the same kind of storm.

This picture shows some of the destruction caused by Cyclone Tracy in Darwin, Australia in 1974. Cyclones and typhoons are the same kind of storms as hurricanes, but they have different names because they start in different parts of the world.

Hurricanes on the move

Once a storm has started, it does not stay in one place. Hurricanes can travel thousands of kilometres over the oceans. They move like a spinning top – spiralling around their **eye** at high speeds. At the same time, the whole storm moves slowly forwards or backwards in another direction. Most hurricanes travel generally west or northwards. The average speed for a hurricane to travel is 10 kilometres an hour.

Hurricanes occur in the **northern hemisphere** and cyclones happen mostly in the **southern hemisphere**. Hurricanes and cyclones usually spin in opposite directions. This is because the Earth is turning slowly all the time. As it turns, it pulls the winds blowing above its surface in different directions. It pulls winds to the right in the northern hemisphere and to the left in the southern hemisphere. This means hurricanes spin anticlockwise and cyclones spin clockwise!

The arrows on this world map show where hurricanes, cyclones and typhoons usually form and the routes that they usually take.

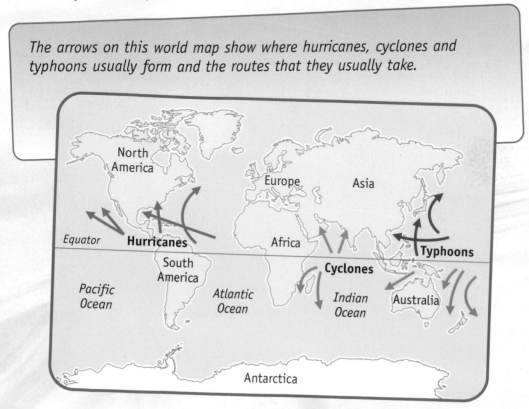

When do hurricanes happen?

Hurricanes happen every year. There has been a hurricane, cyclone or typhoon recorded every year for the past 500 years. It is likely that they happened just as regularly before that, too. Every year there is also at least one major hurricane which reaches land somewhere and causes damage or destruction.

Hurricanes always happen at certain times of the year, known as the **hurricane seasons**. In tropical oceans and seas, like the Gulf of Mexico and the Caribbean Sea, the hurricane season begins in May or June. In the Atlantic Ocean they usually happen from July to October. Hurricane seasons may last up to six months, but the worst storms usually happen over a two-month period – for example, July and August in the eastern Pacific.

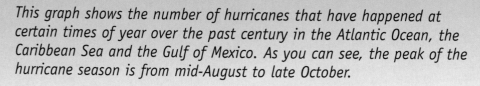

This graph shows the number of hurricanes that have happened at certain times of year over the past century in the Atlantic Ocean, the Caribbean Sea and the Gulf of Mexico. As you can see, the peak of the hurricane season is from mid-August to late October.

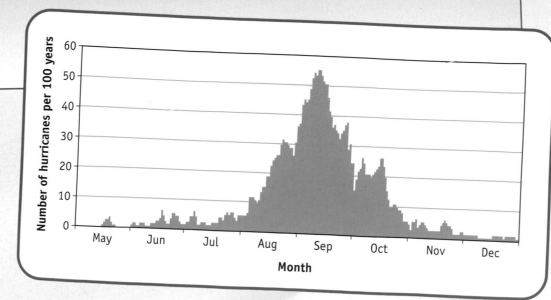

Hurricanes Isidore and Lili, Cuba, 2002

In a **hurricane season**, hurricanes can sometimes strike one after another. In 2002 Hurricane Isidore hit Cuba on 20 September, followed less than two weeks later by Hurricane Lili. Even though most people moved to a safe place before the hurricanes hit, many thousands of houses were damaged or destroyed. The hurricanes also reached Louisiana and Texas on the south-east coast of the USA. By the time they got there they were weaker, but they still caused serious damage.

'Some fishing villages were wiped off the map. People could not take anything with them, so when they returned to their homes everything they had was destroyed.' Cristina Estrada, a worker for the Red Cross, an **aid organization** that helps people in emergencies

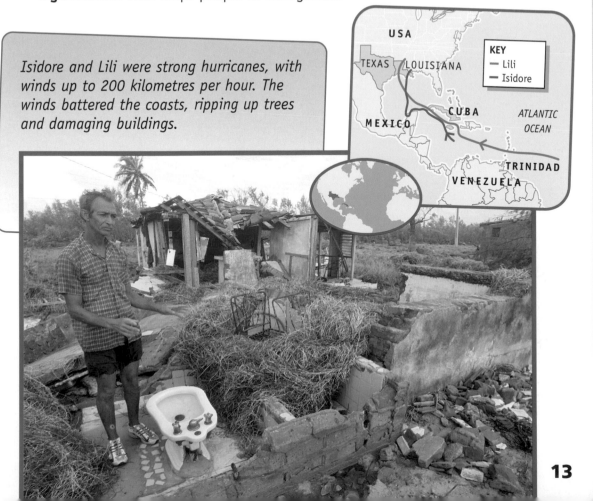

Isidore and Lili were strong hurricanes, with winds up to 200 kilometres per hour. The winds battered the coasts, ripping up trees and damaging buildings.

What happens in a hurricane?

As a hurricane passes directly over people or places, there are three different stages. First, wind builds up, becoming very fast and bringing heavy rain. Then the wind dies down and the rain stops. This is when the calm centre – the **eye** – of the hurricane passes over. This can last for minutes or even hours, as hurricanes sometimes hover over one place. Then, it moves on and the other side of the hurricane passes over, bringing more fierce winds from the opposite direction and rain.

Hurricanes bring heavy showers of rain. These can cause flooding on land. A hurricane's high winds can whip up high waves that crash onto shores. Hurricanes can also cause **tornadoes**.

Many people have died after going outside while the eye of the storm was passing over, because they thought the hurricane was over. To be safe, people should stay in shelters like this one until the storm is completely over.

Tornadoes

Tornadoes can form in thunderstorms and hurricanes. A tornado is a tall funnel of wind that spins very fast. Tornadoes look like a rope of cloud coming down from a storm cloud. They are smaller and even faster than hurricane winds. Unlike hurricanes, tornadoes can travel far across land. This means they pass over more places where people live, causing lots of damage.

What damage do hurricane winds cause?

Hurricane winds are so fast and strong they can move large objects as easily as blowing a hat off your head. Even the weakest hurricane winds can blow tiles off roofs, rattle windows and snap branches. The worst hurricanes can blow down trees and move cars and **mobile homes**.

Strong hurricane winds often knock down electricity and telephone cables. This means people cannot use electric lights or cookers and may not be able to call others for help.

Rain damage

Hurricanes can drop huge amounts of rain over a short period of time. A big hurricane can drop so much rain that it causes floods. Floods are when land that is usually dry becomes covered with water. This can happen when rainwater makes rivers so high that the water spills over the sides and onto the land around it.

When floodwater sweeps through a town or city it can damage buildings and bury houses under mud. It drowns people if they cannot get away in time. When floodwater covers fields of crops it ruins them and it can also drown farm animals. When this happens it can leave people dangerously short of food.

In 1996, Hurricane Fran dropped huge amounts of rain in Alexandria, Virginia, USA. This heavy rainfall caused serious floods across the region.

What is a storm surge?

When a hurricane gets close to land, the winds can push a high wall of water in front of them. This is called a **storm surge**. When this kind of wave hits land it can cause terrible damage to the coastline.

Storm surges can change the whole shape of the land. They may destroy beaches by dragging the sand and rocks out to sea. Sometimes they dump sand and create new beaches. Finally, storm surges can also cover land and cause floods.

HURRICANE ⚡ FACTS

These are things that people should do in a hurricane:

! Stay indoors and keep away from windows.

! If electricity is cut off, use torches to see in the dark. Do not use candles, which can cause fires if they are blown over.

! Listen to radio or TV reports and take the advice given by experts and emergency services.

The combination of winds, rain and storm surges causes terrible damage. In 1996, Hurricane Fran ruined thousands of homes and flattened millions of trees up to 240 kilometres inland from the sea in North Carolina, USA.

Hurricane Andrew, USA, 1992

The first hurricane in the US **hurricane season** of 1992 arrived in southern Florida on 24 August. It was named Hurricane Andrew. Hurricane Andrew's winds were spiralling at about 280 kilometres per hour and it was travelling across land at about 30 kilometres per hour. As it moved over the warm waters of the Gulf of Mexico it gained strength. It only began to weaken as it travelled over land across the state of Louisiana. Hurricane Andrew caused over 60 deaths and huge amounts of damage.

'I've lived through ten hurricanes in my lifetime, and this is going to be the worst. I'm scared. I won't lie to you. I am scared.'
Louisiana cafe worker, Janice Semien

This special picture, taken over a period of four days, shows the movements of Hurricane Andrew between 23 and 26 August 1992.

What damage did Hurricane Andrew cause?

Andrew turned out to be one of America's most expensive hurricanes. Out at sea it churned up high waves, which toppled **oil platforms** and badly damaged **oil wells**. When it passed over coastlines, **storm surges** smashed millions of dollars' worth of boats and ships moored in the water.

Scientists who were following the movements of the hurricane were able to warn people it was coming. About 2 million people were **evacuated** – they left their homes to stay somewhere safer. The hurricane damaged or destroyed houses, **mobile homes**, businesses, bridges and roads. It also badly damaged the Louisiana fishing industry. Over 184 million fish were killed in one area alone!

The buildings and many other structures that Hurricane Andrew damaged or destroyed cost over 20 billion US dollars to mend or rebuild.

Who helps after a hurricane?

After a hurricane has passed over, the danger does not end. Most people who die because of a hurricane drown in floods. Emergency service workers, such as fire rescue workers and the **armed forces**, get people to a safe place.

Other workers, from local hospitals and **aid organizations** like the Red Cross, set up first-aid stations to treat wounds. They also set up shelters where people who have been **evacuated** from their homes can stay. They give **evacuees** blankets, water, food and any medical supplies they need. Emergency workers travel around the area to fix fallen electric power lines that could **electrocute** people, and cut down damaged trees that could fall on them.

Sometimes rescue workers have to lift people out of dangerous fast-flowing flood water caused by hurricanes. This baby was rescued from floods caused by Hurricane Hortense in Puerto Rico in September 1996.

Rich and poor

It takes time to put things back to normal after a hurricane. Bridges and buildings have to be rebuilt or mended. Water companies mend broken **sewage** and water pipes. Government workers clean roads of obstructions such as mud, broken branches and wrecked signs. Generally, people in rich, **developed countries** recover fairly quickly.

In a **developing country**, flooding from a hurricane can cause more long-term suffering. Poorer families usually do not have **insurance** or savings to pay for repairs. If their **crops** are ruined, they may starve. Aid organizations, such as Oxfam, and the governments of other countries send help. They may supply farm equipment, seeds and farm animals. They may also send building equipment, so that people can rebuild their homes themselves.

*Charities make sure that **aid** such as clean water supplies gets to the people who need it most after a hurricane.*

Hurricane Mitch, Central America, 1998

In October 1998 a terrible hurricane raged across Central America. Winds up to 250 kilometres per hour swept through, bringing torrential rains. Hurricane Mitch left over 9000 people dead, many missing and millions more people without homes. Roads and bridges were wrecked by the storm. Floods ruined farmland, many **crops** and people's food stores. Heavy rains caused **landslides** too. A landslide is when mud and rock slide down a hill causing great damage.

'Some neighbourhoods were flooded by water up to 1.5 metres high. People screamed asking for help and some of us, helped by tyre inner-tubes, threw ourselves in [the water] to rescue those trapped in their homes.' Roberto Ramos, a Honduran nurse

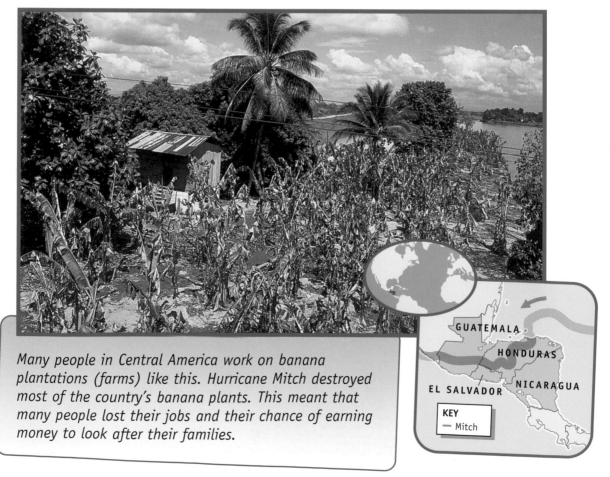

Many people in Central America work on banana plantations (farms) like this. Hurricane Mitch destroyed most of the country's banana plants. This meant that many people lost their jobs and their chance of earning money to look after their families.

GUATEMALA
HONDURAS
EL SALVADOR
NICARAGUA
KEY
— Mitch

Long-term support

At first, **aid organizations** such as Oxfam and the Red Cross helped by giving people food, water, medical treatment and somewhere to stay. They also helped people find family members who got lost in all the chaos.

Later their main aim was to get farms working again. That way people could feed themselves, without having to rely on help from other people. **Aid** organizations worked with local groups to plan what to do. Gradually, they helped people grow new corn, rice, bean and banana plants to eat and sell. The poorest people in the area were the worst affected. Their houses were flimsy and had been completely wrecked by the hurricane. Aid organizations helped people build new, stronger homes, as well as new wells, bridges and roads.

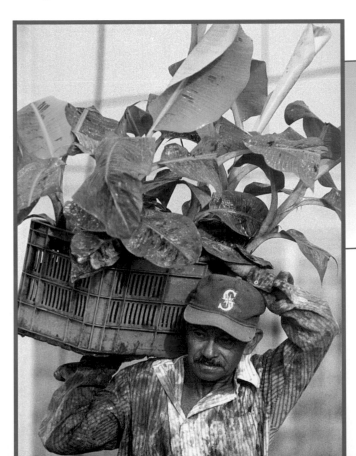

Many banana plantations had to be replanted with baby banana plants after the entire crop was destroyed by Hurricane Mitch.

Can hurricanes be predicted?

Predicting hurricanes is difficult because each one grows and moves differently. Some countries spend a lot of money on **scientists** and equipment to try to work out when and where hurricanes might happen. If they can work out where a hurricane is heading, they can tell people in that area to **evacuate**.

Satellite pictures

Weather **satellites** are special computers that are sent out into space. From space they photograph the clouds high above the Earth. This helps scientists on Earth to predict the weather. Hurricane experts study these pictures to see if there are any clouds that look like they could become hurricanes. They also use powerful supercomputers. These examine weather and hurricane information from around the world to help them with their predictions.

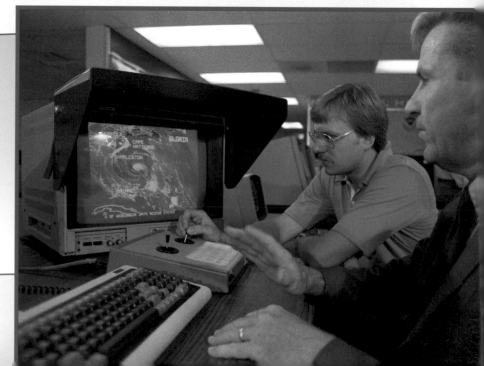

These scientists at the US National Hurricane Center are using a computer-enhanced satellite photo to track the progress of a hurricane as it approaches the USA.

Hurricane hunters

When dangerous-looking storm clouds are spotted, hurricane hunters go to look at them. These people fly planes all around and into storms and hurricanes. They have special equipment to take measurements and pictures of the weather inside the storm.

For example, they drop miniature weather stations into a hurricane's **eyewall** on a parachute. This measures things like temperature, **humidity** and wind speed. It sends the information to experts' computers. The experts look at this information along with satellite pictures and facts about the way that hurricanes in the past grew. This helps them to work out how strong a hurricane is and which way it is likely to go.

*The hurricane hunters in this plane are part of the United States Air Force. Hurricane hunters are skilled pilots who fly right into the **eyes** of storms and hurricanes. They may stay in the air for up to fourteen hours at a time!*

Can people prepare for hurricanes?

When **scientists** predict a hurricane, they send out warnings on TV and radio. If it is a very dangerous hurricane this gives people time to **evacuate**. If it is a weaker hurricane this gives people time to prepare for the storm. Most people who live in areas where there is a danger of hurricanes make some preparations in advance.

Long-term preparations

People can do several things to make their houses safer. For example, they can fix strong shutters to their windows. When these are closed, they stop hurricane winds shattering the glass. People also cut down dead branches or trees. In hurricanes these can cause a lot of damage when they snap off and blow about.

*Before a **hurricane season**, some governments advise people to stock up on essential supplies. Items include tinned foods, batteries for torches and portable radios, bottled water and a first-aid kit.*

Governments can prepare for hurricanes further ahead, when planning new structures such as buildings and bridges. They can make stronger buildings that can cope with strong wind and rain. They can put important buildings, such as hospitals, further inland where they are safer from hurricanes. They can also build bigger storm drains that allow large amounts of water to soak away. This means that future floods will not be so deep.

HURRICANE ⚡ FACTS

If a hurricane is on its way, but not one strong enough that people need to evacuate, there are still a number of steps that they should take:

- People should check their portable radio has batteries.

- They should bring in or tie down loose objects outside, such as garden furniture.

- They should close windows and shutters.

- They should move food and other supplies into the basement or cellar (or the lowest room of the house) where people will be during the storm.

It is important that all animals are safe inside too. These flamingos from Miami Zoo, USA, are sheltering from a hurricane in one of the zoo toilets!

Can hurricanes be prevented?

People have tried to prevent hurricanes in the past. In 1947, **scientists** tried to weaken a hurricane over water near America. They flew planes into the storm and dropped dry ice into the clouds to try to cool and calm it before it reached the shore. It did not work! Scientists today are working on new ideas, but we may never be able to stop hurricanes.

Scientists have learned a great deal about how hurricanes work. This is important, especially when more and more people are building homes near coastlines. Although it is impossible to predict all hurricanes, tracking and warning systems can help to save lives. They give people time to escape and lessen the damage these awesome forces of nature can cause.

In 1935 a hurricane hit Florida Keys, USA, killing around 408 people. In 1960 Hurricane Donna (right) hit the same area. Even though many more people were living there, early warnings meant that only three people died this time.

Howling hurricanes of the past

1900, Galveston Hurricane
Storm-surge waves 4.5 metres high swamped the whole of Galveston city and parts of the Texas coast in the USA. Around 8000 people died.

1926, Great Miami Hurricane
This storm caused over 100 million US dollars of damage in Florida, USA. If the same storm were to happen today it would cause 80 billion US dollars of damage because there are so many more people living in Florida now!

1944, Great Atlantic Hurricane
This major hurricane hit the eastern US coast. Over 20 centimetres of rain and 200-kilometre-per-hour winds caused 46 deaths.

1969, Hurricane Camille
Huge floods struck after as much as 70 centimetres of rain fell in 5 hours when this hurricane hit the Mississippi Gulf Coast, USA, killing 250 people.

1974, Cyclone Tracy
This hurricane hit Darwin, Australia, on Christmas Day morning, 1974. A total of 50 people were killed and 112 more were seriously injured. Around 90 per cent of the city was damaged.

1974, Hurricane Fifi
This hurricane devastated large areas of Honduras in Central America. Over 60,000 people were left homeless and 8000 died.

1979, Hurricane David
This hurricane caused over 1 billion US dollars' worth of damage to Dominica and the Dominican Republic in the Caribbean.

1979, Typhoon Tip
This awesome typhoon was at least 1000 kilometres across, with wind speeds over 300 kilometres per hour. Luckily, Typhoon Tip never directly hit land.

1984, Typhoon Ike
Over a million people were made homeless after Typhoon Ike hit the Philippines.

Glossary

aid help given as money, medicine, food or other essential items

aid organizations groups that raise money and provide help for people in need

armed forces army, air force and navy. These forces have equipment to fight with but also help rescue people at other times.

crops plants grown to eat and to sell, such as rice and bananas

developed countries richer countries of the world that have well-developed services for their people, such as good hospitals and emergency services

developing countries poorer countries of the world that are gradually developing better conditions for their people

electrocute injure or kill with electricity

Equator imaginary line around the centre of the Earth

evacuate when people move from a dangerous place to somewhere safe

evacuee someone who moves from a dangerous place to somewhere safe

evaporate when water turns from liquid into a vapour (a gas in the air)

eye calm centre of a hurricane

eyewall edge of the eye of a hurricane

humidity when the weather is very warm and moist at the same time

hurricane season some areas have hurricanes every year at about the same time. This is called the hurricane season.

insurance when people pay money regularly to a company that pays the full cost of rebuilding their home or business if it is damaged or destroyed

landslides when heavy rains and wind make large amounts of mud and rock slide down a hill or mountain

mobile home home that can be moved using lorries. Most mobile homes look a bit like big caravans without wheels.

northern hemisphere everywhere on the Earth north of the Equator

oil platform/well an oil platform is a building at sea around an oil well. An oil well is a deep narrow hole drilled to release oil found underground.

rotate spin or turn around

satellite object in space that sends out TV signals or takes photographs

scientists people who study aspects of the world around us

sewage waste from lavatories

southern hemisphere everywhere on the Earth south of the Equator

storm surge when the sea becomes high along a coast due to storm winds

tornadoes strong whirlwinds that move quickly over land

tropical in the tropics – regions around the Equator that have hot and humid weather

Find out more

Books

DK Eyewitness Guides: Hurricane and Tornado, Jack Challoner (Dorling Kindersley, 2000)

DK Guide to Weather, Michael Allaby (Dorling Kindersley, 2000)

Hurricanes and Tornadoes, Neil Morris (Crabtree Pub Co., 1998)

Natural Disasters: Hurricanes and Typhoons, J. Dineen (Franklin Watts, 2002)

Storms, Mark Maslin (Hodder Children's Books, 2000)

Wild Weather: Thunderstorm, Catherine Chambers (Heinemann Library, 2002)

Websites

www.howstuffworks.com/hurricane.htm – to find out more about how hurricanes work go to the hurricane pages.

www.nhc.noaa.gov – read up about America's national hurricane centre if you want to know more about tracking hurricanes.

www.fema.gov/hazards/hurricanes – for facts about hurricane dangers, what to do and how to prepare.

Disclaimer
All the Internet addresses (URLs) given in this book were valid at the time of going to press. However, due to the dynamic nature of the Internet, some addresses may have changed, or sites may have changed or ceased to exist since publication. While the author and publishers regret any inconvenience this may cause readers, no responsibility for any such changes can be accepted by either the author or the publishers.

Index

Titles in the *Awesome Forces of Nature* series include:

Hardback   0 431 17828 3

Hardback   0 431 17831 3

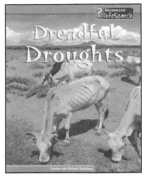

Hardback   0 431 17829 1

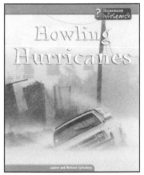

Hardback   0 431 17835 6

Hardback   0 431 17830 5

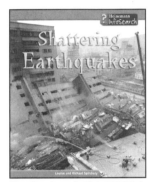

Hardback   0 431 17836 4

Hardback   0 431 17832 1

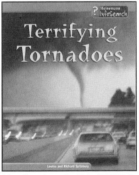

Hardback   0 431 17837 2

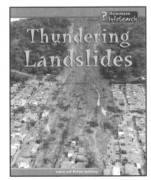

Hardback   0 431 17838 0

Hardback   0 431 17834 8

Find out about the other titles in this series on our website
www.heinemann.co.uk/library